W9-BYR-525

Quilted Gifts From Your Scraps & Stash™

Editor **Carolyn Vagts**
Creative Director **Brad Snow**
Publishing Services Director **Brenda Gallmeyer**

Editorial Assistants **Sharon Frank,**
Carol Listenberger
Graphic Designer **Nick Pierce**
Copy Supervisor **Deborah Morgan**
Copy Editors **Emily Carter, Samantha Schneider**
Technical Editor **Angie Buckles**
Technical Proofreader **Sandra L. Hatch**
Technical Artist **Debera Kuntz**

Production Artist Supervisor **Erin Brandt**
Senior Production Artist **Nicole Gage**
Production Artists **Glenda Chamberlain,**
Edith Teegarden
Production Assistants **Marj Morgan,**
Judy Neuenschwander

Photography Supervisor **Tammy Christian**
Photography **Matthew Owen, Shane Pequinot**
Photography Assistants **Tammy Liechty,**
Tammy Steiner

Quilted Gifts From Your Scraps & Stash is published by Annie's, 306 East Parr Road, Berne, IN 46711. Printed in USA. Copyright © 2012, 2013 Annie's. All rights reserved. This publication may not be reproduced in part or in whole without written permission from the publisher.

RETAIL STORES: If you would like to carry this book or any other Annie's publication, visit AnniesWSL.com

Every effort has been made to ensure that the instructions in this pattern book are complete and accurate. We cannot, however, take responsibility for human error, typographical mistakes or variations in individual work. Please visit AnniesCustomerCare.com to check for pattern updates.

Library of Congress Control Number: 2011931328
Softcover ISBN: 978-1-59217-366-2

4 5 6 7 8 9 10

Welcome

As a quilter, there are many times you need or want to make a gift for someone, someone with very different tastes from your own. These are the times when a book with a wide range of projects and varied completion times would be extremely handy. A book from which you could find the right project for the occasion and, even better yet, be able to use your stash and scraps to complete it.

Quilted Gifts From Your Scraps & Stash is the book you have been looking for. Turn your scraps and stash into fabulous gifts for everyone on your list and for every occasion. This book is destined to be a favorite that is used time and time again. It has such a wide range of projects, and the beauty of this publication is that it not only uses your scraps, it divides the projects by the time it will take to complete them. If you are in a hurry, chapter one, 5-Hour Favorites, is what you will want to check out first. If time is not a consideration, go to chapter five, Take Your Time.

If you are looking for a great project book with a lot of variety, this is it. Although this book is full of great gift-giving projects, that is not its sole purpose. It has something for everyone, especially you.

Carolyn L. Vagts

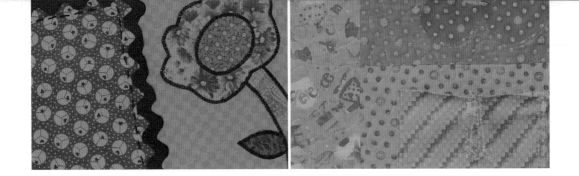

Contents

5-Hour Favorites

4 Pocket Full of Posies
7 Charming Coasters
10 Halloween Treat Bags
15 Granny's Hanky
18 Butterfly Pot Holder
22 Fruit Quartet Pot Holders
27 Sassy Slide
30 Christmas Card Holder
34 Quick Mug Rugs
36 Strip-Pieced Place Mats
38 Mini Dresden Ornament

10-Hour Treats

42 Ruffled Rose Pillow
46 Chair Chatelaine
50 Simply Scrappy Place Mats
53 Wild Goose Chase Tote
58 Wild Goose Chase Wallet
64 Cracker Box
68 May Day Tulip Place Mat
74 Daisy Pocket Quilt
79 Cellphone Carrier

17-Hour Sensations

83 Color Wheel Runner
87 Jolly Santa Pot Holder
90 Pathways Prayer Shawl
94 Dots Done Your Way
98 Black Lily Bag
102 E-Reader Tech Bag
106 3-D Drunkard's Path Quilt
110 Log Cabin Doll Quilt

24-Hour Treasures

114 Batiks Squared
118 Button Checkerboard
122 Twisted Rail Fence
126 Sleepytime Lambs Baby Quilt
132 Magic Maze
136 Friendship Stars Backpack
140 Diamond Candy

Take Your Time

145 Puppy Dog Tails
154 Windflowers
160 Skins & Stones Throw
166 Skins & Sticks Pillow
170 3-D Tumbling Blocks

174 Photo Gallery
176 Fabric & Supplies
176 Special Thanks

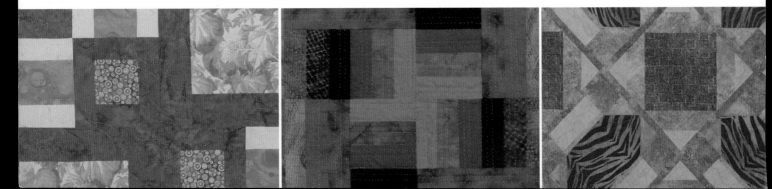

5-Hour Favorites

If you need a great gift that takes just an afternoon to complete, you'll love these 5-Hour Favorites. This chapter of *Quilted Gifts From Your Scraps and Stash* includes Charming Coasters, Halloween Treat Bags, Granny's Hanky and a wide variety of additional projects that will delight children and adults alike. And the best part is that you can make these lovely treasures from smaller scraps and your stash of fabric that you have been saving for a special project!

Pocket Full of Posies

Bold, black rickrack adds power and action to rather quiet reproduction pastels.

DESIGN BY BETH WHEELER

PROJECT SPECIFICATIONS

Skill Level: Beginner
Pillow Size: 20" x 20"

MATERIALS

- Light or medium pink, yellow, lavender, green and peach print scraps, at least 6" square
- 4 fat quarters assorted medium blue prints
- Backing 2 (15" x 20") pieces
- 20" square pillow form
- 20" square fusible fleece
- 1 package jumbo black rickrack
- ¼ yard paper-backed fusible web
- ½ yard fabric stabilizer
- Black and natural all-purpose thread
- Black machine-embroidery thread
- Black 6-strand embroidery floss
- Basic sewing tools & supplies

Cutting

1. Cut one 5½" A square from each light pink, yellow, lavender and peach print scraps.

2. Cut a total of five 5½" B squares, two 3" x 15½" C strips and two 3" x 20½" D strips from the medium blue prints.

3. Trace appliqué shapes on paper side of fusible web as directed on patterns for number to trace, leaving ½" between shapes. Cut out, leaving approximately ¼" margin around each shape.

4. Following manufacturer's directions, fuse shapes to fabrics indicated on pattern. Cut out on traced lines.

Completing the Pillow Top

1. Referring to Figure 1, position and fuse appliqué pieces on A squares and one B square.

Figure 1

2. Using fabric stabilizer and black machine-embroidery thread, stitch around each shape with medium-wide zigzag or narrow buttonhole stitch; press.

3. Sew a plain A square between two appliquéd A squares as shown in Figure 2. Repeat to make the top and bottom rows. Press seams in one direction.

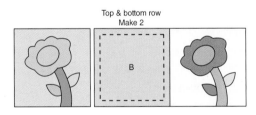

Top & bottom row
Make 2

Figure 2

4. Sew an appliquéd A square between two plain B squares to make the center row (Figure 3). Press seams in opposite direction from top and bottom rows in step 3.

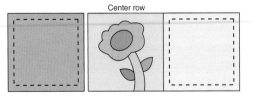

Center row

Figure 3

5. To complete pillow top, refer to the Placement Diagram and sew the center row between the top and bottom rows matching seams. Press seams in one direction.

6. Sew B borders to top and bottom of pieced center. Sew C borders to opposite sides of pieced center to complete pillow top. Press seams toward borders.

7. Following manufacturer's instructions, center and fuse fusible fleece to wrong side of pillow top.

8. With black all-purpose thread, center and stitch rickrack on all seam allowances referring to the Placement Diagram.

9. Sew running stitches around medium blue A blocks that are not appliquéd with 4 strands of black embroidery floss about ⅛" from rickrack.

Completing the Pillow

1. Turn and press ¼" to wrong side of 20" side of a backing piece. Turn and press again ¼" to wrong side. Edgestitch first fold to make a double-turned ¼" hem (Figure 4). Repeat with second backing piece.

Figure 4

2. Position and pin backing pieces right sides together with quilted front; matching raw edges and overlapping (Figure 5). Stitch all edges.

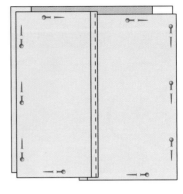

Figure 5

3. Trim batting close to stitching and corners. Turn right side out and press seams. Insert pillow form to complete. ■

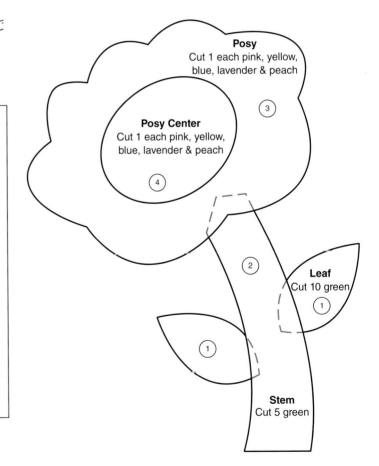

Posy
Cut 1 each pink, yellow, blue, lavender & peach

③

Posy Center
Cut 1 each pink, yellow, blue, lavender & peach

④

②

Leaf
Cut 10 green

①

①

Stem
Cut 5 green

Pocket Full of Posies
Placement Diagram 20" x 20"

Charming Coasters

Making these fun coasters is a wonderful way to use up those leftover 5-inch charm squares making quick, easy and thoughtful hostess gifts.

DESIGN BY CHRIS MALONE

PROJECT SPECIFICATIONS

Skill Level: Beginner
Coaster Size: 4½" x 4½"
Number of Coasters: 4

MATERIALS

- 12 coordinating 5" x 5" squares
- 4 (5" x 5") batting squares
- 2 yards coordinating-color medium rickrack
- ¼ yard fusible web
- All-purpose thread to match fabrics
- Contrasting-color size 8 or 16 pearl cotton
- Basic sewing tools and supplies

Cutting

1. Select four 5" squares for A coaster fronts, four for B backs and four to make circle appliqués.

2. Cut circle appliqué squares into four 2½" C squares each.

3. Cut four 6" lengths of coordinating-color medium rickrack.

Completing the Coasters

1. Select one 2½" C square from each of the circle appliqué squares; join the two C squares to make a row (Figure 1). Repeat to make two rows. Press seams in opposite directions.

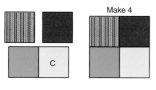

Figure 1

2. Join the rows to make a Four-Patch square, again referring to Figure 1. Press seam open.

3. Repeat steps 1 and 2 to make four Four-Patch squares.

4. Draw four 3½"-diameter circles on paper side of fusible web, leaving ½" between shapes. Cut out circles, leaving a ¼" margin around each one. Fold fusible-web circles into quarters to mark vertical and horizontal centers.

5. Arrange a fusible-web circle on wrong side of a Four-Patch square, matching seam lines to creased centers (Figure 2).

Figure 2

6. Follow manufacturer's instructions to bond the fusible-web circle to the wrong side of the Four-Patch square. Cut on drawn lines to make Four-Patch circle; remove paper backing.

7. Fold and press A square in half vertically and horizontally. Center and fuse the circle to A, matching fold lines of A to seams of Four-Patch circle.

8. Use a narrow machine blanket stitch or zigzag stitch to sew around the circle to complete the appliqué on the coaster front.

9. Repeat steps 5–8 to make four coaster fronts.

10. Baste a 6" length of coordinating-color medium rickrack to the right-side edge of each coaster front (Figure 3).

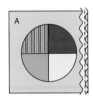

Figure 3

11. Layer the coaster front with a B square right sides together on a 5" square of batting. Stitch together ¼" from edges, leaving a 2" opening along one plain side (Figure 4).

batting

2"

Figure 4

12. Clip corners and trim batting close to stitching (Figure 5); turn coaster right side out and press.

batting

Figure 5

13. Fold opening seam allowance to inside and hand-stitch opening closed.

14. Topstitch close to outer edges.

15. Hand-quilt around each circle and ⅛" away with contrasting-color size 8 or 16 pearl cotton using a ⅛"-long stitch to finish (Figure 6). ■

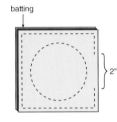
⅛"

Figure 6

Charm Coasters
Placement Diagram 4½" x 4½"

Halloween Treat Bags

Halloween has never been so cute. These bags are sure to get your little ghosts and goblins the treats they deserve.

DESIGN BY CHRIS MALONE

PROJECT SPECIFICATIONS

Skill Level: Beginner
Bag Size: 12" x 12", excluding handle and ears

CAT BAG
MATERIALS

- 2"-diameter circle scrap orange tonal
- ½ yard black tonal
- ½ yard Halloween print
- 1 package craft-size batting (34" x 45") or scraps
- Black all-purpose thread
- White and black size 8 pearl cotton
- ½ yard ⅜"-wide orange Halloween ribbon
- 1 (1") shank button, any color
- 2 (1⅛") white 4-hole buttons
- White marking pencil
- 20" length black knit cord
- Craft glue
- No-fray solution
- 12½" paper square
- Dinner plate
- Embroidery needle
- Basic sewing tools and supplies

Cutting

1. Prepare ear template using pattern given. Cut as directed on pattern.

2. Make a bag pattern by folding and creasing the 12½" paper square in half. Using a dinner plate, mark and trim the folded paper to make curved bottom corners as shown in Figure 1.

3. Use the bag pattern to cut a bag front and back from the black tonal and Halloween print and two batting pieces.

4. Cut two 3½" squares and one 1"-diameter circle from batting.

12½"

Figure 1

Completing the Cat Bag

1. Pin the bag front to one batting piece; machine-baste ³⁄₁₆" from the edge. Repeat with the bag back and remaining batting piece.

2. Transfer the whiskers and centerline from the cat face positioning pattern to the cat bag front.

3. Use an embroidery needle and 1 strand of white pearl cotton to sew long quilting stitches on the marked lines.

4. Place two ear pieces right sides together and pin to the batting ears; stitch all around, leaving bottom edge of ear open. Trim batting close to seam; clip off tip. Turn right side out and press flat. Repeat to make second ear.

5. Hand-stitch ¼" from seam on each ear using white pearl cotton and referring to step 3.

6. Place the ears at the top of the cat bag front ¾" from corners as shown in Figure 2; baste in place.

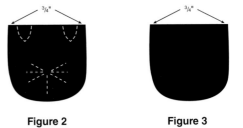

Figure 2   **Figure 3**

7. Place the cut ends of the cord at the top edge of the right side of the bag back ¾" from corners; baste in place referring to Figure 3.

8. Sew one lining piece right sides together with the bag front at the top straight edges as shown in Figure 4; repeat with the second lining piece and the bag back. Open the pieces as shown in Figure 5.

Figure 4

Figure 5

9. Layer the two units right sides together with the lining at one end and the bag front and back at the other end. Sew all around, leaving a 5" opening along one side of the lining as shown in Figure 6; clip curves and turn right side out through the opening. Press edges flat.

Figure 6

10. Fold the opening seam allowances to the inside ¼"; hand-stitch opening closed.

11. Push the lining down inside the bag, pulling ears and cord up and out; press top edge flat.

12. Topstitch all around the top of the bag ¼" from the edge.

13. Glue the 1" batting circle to the top of the shank button. Sew gathering stitches around the edge of orange tonal circle; place the button, batting side down, in the center of the wrong side of the circle. Pull the threads to gather the fabric around the button as shown in Figure 7; knot and clip the thread to make the nose.

Figure 7

14. Center the nose on the cat's face and stitch in place through the bag front and front lining using black pearl cotton.

15. Sew the 1⅛" white buttons in place for eyes using black pearl cotton.

16. Tie the orange ribbon into a bow and tack to the front of the bag by one ear. Apply no-fray solution to the ribbon ends to finish.

FRANKENSTEIN BAG
MATERIALS

- 2½"-diameter scrap purple dot
- Scrap coordinating stripe
- Fat eighth purple tonal
- ½ yard green tonal
- ½ yard Halloween print
- 1 package craft-size batting (34" x 45") or scraps
- Neutral-color all-purpose thread
- Black size 8 pearl cotton
- 2 (1¼") 4-hole buttons, any color
- 6" length large black rickrack
- ⅛ yard fusible web
- Water soluble marking pen
- 20" length black knit cord
- Craft glue
- No-fray solution
- 12½" paper square
- Dinner plate
- Embroidery needle
- Basic sewing tools and supplies

Cutting

1. Using the paper pattern made in step 2 of the Cat Bag cutting instructions, cut a bag front and back from the green tonal and Halloween print and two batting pieces.

2. Draw two 2¼" x 1" eyebrow rectangles and one 5" x 1¼" mouth rectangle on the paper side of the fusible web, leaving at least ¼" between pieces. Cut out shapes, leaving a margin around each one.

3. Fuse the 2¼" x 1" eyebrow rectangles to the wrong side of the stripe with stripes going horizontally and the 5" x 1¼" mouth rectangle with stripes going vertically. Cut out shapes and remove paper backing.

4. Cut four 2½" x 3½" rectangles from the purple tonal for ears.

5. Cut two 2½" x 3½" rectangles and two 1¼"-diameter circles from batting.

Completing the Frankenstein Bag

1. Place the rickrack across the center of the mouth rectangle, trim to fit and apply no-fray solution to the ends; let dry. Stitch down the center of the rickrack to secure.

2. Position the eyebrow and mouth pieces on the bag front piece; fuse in place.

3. Pin the bag front to one batting piece; machine-baste ³⁄₁₆" from the edge. Repeat with the bag back and remaining batting piece.

4. Transfer the eye, nose and chin quilting lines to the bag front referring to the Frankenstein face positioning pattern. Using an embroidery needle and 1 strand of black pearl cotton, sew long quilting stitches along the marked lines.

5. Place two ear rectangles right sides together and pin to a 2½" x 3½" batting rectangle. Sew around, leaving one long edge open. Trim batting close to seam; clip corners. Turn right side out and press flat. Repeat for second ear.

6. Using black pearl cotton, sew long quilting stitches ¾" from the seam.

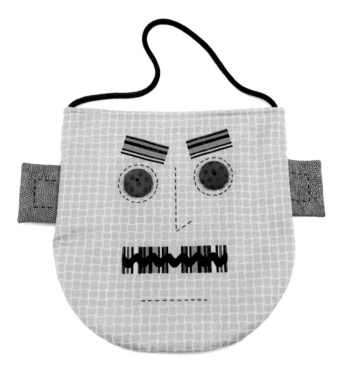

7. Place the ears at the sides of the bag front with one ear 3½" down from the top and the other 4" down; baste in place as shown in Figure 8.

Figure 8

8. Refer to steps 7–12 in Completing the Cat Bag to sew the bag together.

9. Glue the 1¼"-diameter batting circles to the top of two buttons.

10. Sew gathering stitches around the edge of each circle and place a button, batting side down, in the center of the wrong side of each purple dot circle. Pull the threads to gather the fabric around the button, referring to Figure 7 on page 11; knot and clip the thread.

11. Center a button inside each quilted eye circle on the bag front and stitch in place using black pearl cotton, stitching through the holes in the button and the bag front and front lining to finish. ■

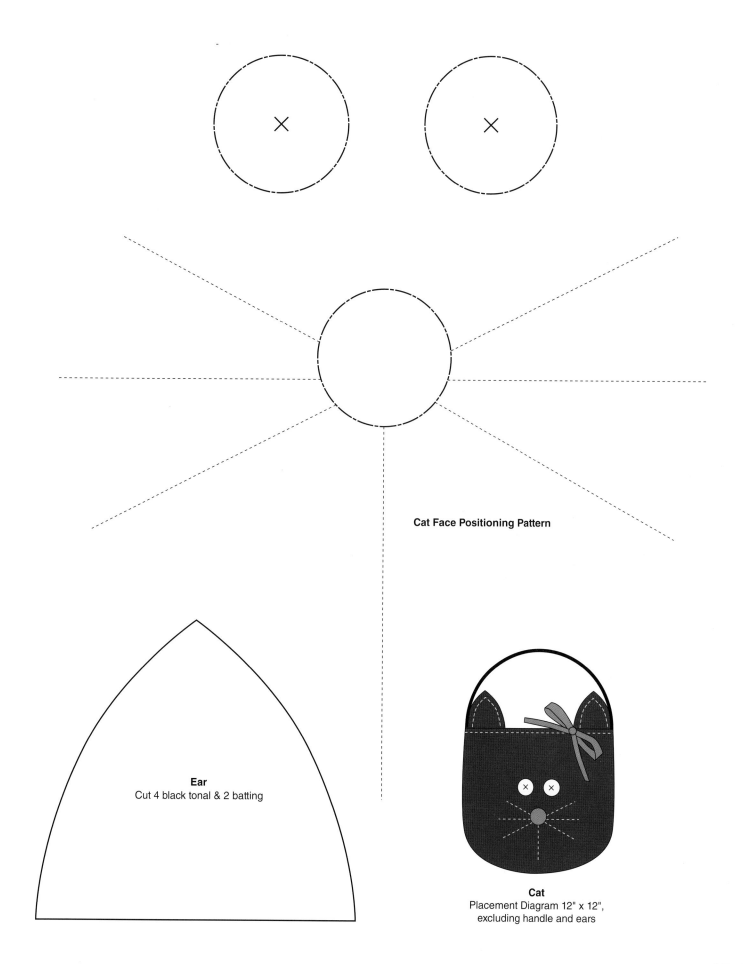

Cat Face Positioning Pattern

Ear
Cut 4 black tonal & 2 batting

Cat
Placement Diagram 12" x 12",
excluding handle and ears

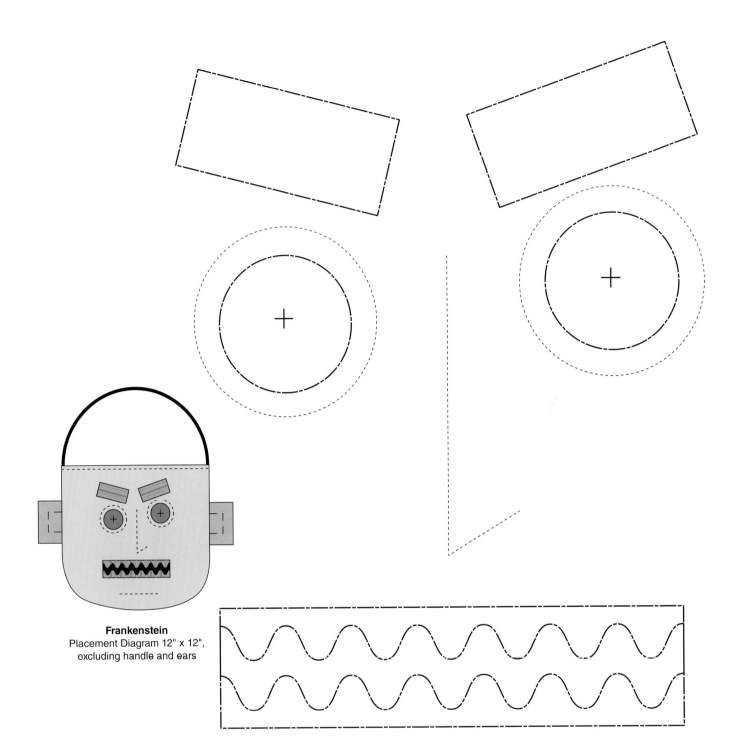

Frankenstein
Placement Diagram 12" x 12",
excluding handle and ears

Frankenstein Face Positioning Pattern

Granny's Hanky

Use one of your grandmother's handkerchiefs to frame her photo in a treasured wall quilt.

DESIGN BY JEAN BOYD

PROJECT SPECIFICATIONS

Skill Level: Beginner
Quilt Size: Size varies

MATERIALS

- 1 new or vintage handkerchief 8" or 12"
- 1 (11" x 14") photo printable fabric
- ¼ yard complementary binding fabric
- ½ yard complementary border fabric
- Batting 3" larger all around than completed top size
- Backing 3" larger all around than completed top size
- Neutral color all-purpose thread
- Quilting thread
- Machine-embroidery thread to contrast or match handkerchief
- 1 square lightweight fusible web, 1" larger all around than handkerchief
- 1 square lightweight fusible interfacing, 1" larger all around than handkerchief
- Basic sewing tools and supplies

Completing the Project

1. Select a favorite vintage handkerchief, preferably one with a border all around the outside edge and an unprinted area in the center as shown in Photo 1.

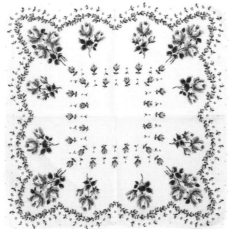

Photo 1

2. Cut one square of lightweight fusible interfacing the same size as the handkerchief.

3. Following the manufacturer's instructions, fuse the interfacing to the wrong side of the handkerchief.

4. Use an ink-jet printer to print a favorite photo on a printable fabric sheet referring to manufacturer's instructions. ***Note:*** *A photo-transfer product may be used if an ink-jet printer is not available.*

Photo 2

5. Trim the photo to leave a ¼" fabric border around the outside edge as shown in Photo 2.

6. Use the trimmed fabric photo as a pattern to cut a square of lightweight fusible web; fuse the web to the wrong side of the fabric photo. Remove paper backing.

7. Trim the photo to eliminate the ¼" fabric border.

8. Fold the interfaced handkerchief in half vertically and horizontally to find the center and crease; repeat with fabric photo creasing lightly on just the outside edges.

9. Iron the photo to the center of the handkerchief using creased lines as guides for placement.

10. Using a machine blanket or buttonhole stitch and machine-embroidery thread, stitch all around the fused photo as shown in Photo 3. ***Note:*** *You may hand-stitch around the photo using 2 or 3 strands of contrasting or matching embroidery floss, if desired.*

Photo 3

11. Measure across the top of the stitched unit. From the complementary border fabric, cut two 2½"-wide A border strips this size and stitch to the top and bottom of the stitched unit; press seams toward A strips.

12. Measure along the side of the stitched unit; cut two B strips the side measurement from the complementary border fabric and stitch to opposite sides; press seams toward B strips.

Completing the Quilt

1. Press quilt top on both sides; check for proper seam pressing and trim all loose threads.

2. Sandwich batting between the stitched top and the prepared backing piece; pin or baste layers together to hold. Quilt on marked lines and as desired by hand or machine.

3. When quilting is complete, remove pins or basting. Trim batting and backing fabric edges even with raw edges of quilt top.

4. Join binding strips on short ends with diagonal seams to make one long strip; trim seams to ¼" and press seams open.

5. Fold the binding strip in half with wrong sides together along length; press.

6. Cut one 4" by the finished width measurement minus 1" from the complementary border fabric for a hanging sleeve.

7. Fold each short end of the hanging-sleeve strip ¼" to wrong side and press. Fold in ¼" again and stitch. Fold the strip in half lengthwise wrong sides together; press.

8. Cut two 3" by fabric width strips from the complementary binding fabric. Position the raw edges of the hanging sleeve even with the raw edge of the top back before binding as shown in Figure 1.

Figure 1

9. Sew binding to quilt edges, matching raw edges, mitering corners and overlapping ends.

10. Fold binding to the back side and stitch in place to finish.

11. Hand-stitch the loose edge of the hanging sleeve to the quilt back to finish. ■

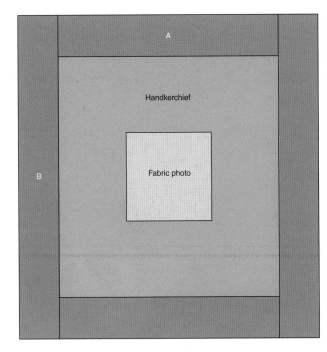

Granny's Hanky
Placement Diagram Size Varies

Butterfly Pot Holder

In five hours or less, stitch this fun, decorative pot holder. Blanket stitching adds a finishing touch to this gift.

DESIGN BY CHRIS MALONE

PROJECT SPECIFICATIONS

Skill Level: Beginner
Pot Holder Size: 7¾" x 9"

MATERIALS

- 1 fat quarter black with orange dots
- 1 (9" x 9") scrap orange solid
- 2 (8" x 5") scraps coordinating orange prints
- 1 (8" x 8") piece paper-backed fusible web
- Insul-bright batting 9" x 9" (or 2 (9") squares cotton batting)
- Black and coordinating with prints size 8 pearl cotton
- All-purpose thread to match fabrics
- Dark orange hand-quilting thread
- 2 (3mm) black beads
- Fiberfill stuffing
- Basic sewing tools and supplies

Cutting

1. Prepare templates from patterns on page 21 for butterfly wings, large and small wing spots and butterfly body, transferring pattern marks to templates.

2. Trace butterfly wing onto right side of orange solid and set aside (Figure 1).

Figure 1

3. Trace large and small wing spots onto paper side of fusible web ½" apart. Cut out, leaving a margin around each piece.

4. Following manufacturer's instructions, fuse a large wing spot to one coordinating orange print and the small wing spot to second coordinating orange print.

5. Cut out on traced lines and remove fusible web backing paper.

6. Cut one butterfly body and one 9" square for backing from black with orange dots.

Completing Butterfly Wings

1. Arrange and fuse first the small wing spot and then large wing spot onto orange solid wings referring to appliqué motif on page 21 and Placement Diagram.

2. Using coordinating-color pearl cotton, hand-sew a blanket stitch around each of the spots referring to Figure 2.

Figure 2

3. Cut out butterfly wings on the traced lines referring to Figure 3.

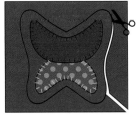

Figure 3

4. Position 9" black with orange dots backing square right side up on the shiny side of the 9" Insul-bright batting square.

5. Center and pin butterfly wings, right side down, on the backing square.

6. Stitch ¼" from the edge around the butterfly wings, leaving a 3" opening at the top for turning (Figure 4).

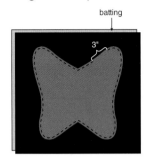

Figure 4

7. Trim batting and backing to match butterfly wings, trimming batting close to stitching and clipping curves referring to Figure 5.

Figure 5

8. Turn butterfly wings right side out through opening and press. Turn opening seam allowance to inside and hand-stitch closed.

9. Machine-stitch down the center of butterfly wings.

10. Hand-stitch a blanket stitch around the outside edges of the butterfly wings using black pearl cotton.

11. Use dark orange thread and a running stitch to hand-quilt around the wing spots referring to Figure 6.

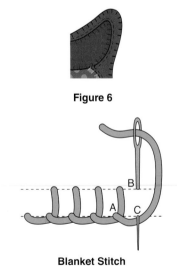

Figure 6

Blanket Stitch

Completing the Hot Pad

1. Fold the butterfly body in half lengthwise with right sides together. Stitch body together, leaving bottom straight edges open for turning (Figure 7).

Figure 7

2. Trim body tip and turn right side out through opening.

3. Firmly stuff the butterfly body with fiberfill. Turn opening edges to inside and hand-stitch closed.

4. Stitch a black bead to each side of the pointed end, at positions marked on pattern, for eyes.

5. Fold the wings in half, right sides out, and match the body seam to the center stitched line on the wings. Using doubled thread, attach the body to the wings between marks referring to Figure 8 to complete the pot holder. ◼

Figure 8

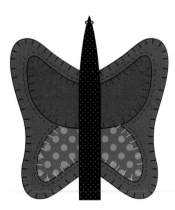

Butterfly Pot Holder
Placement Diagram 7¾" x 9"

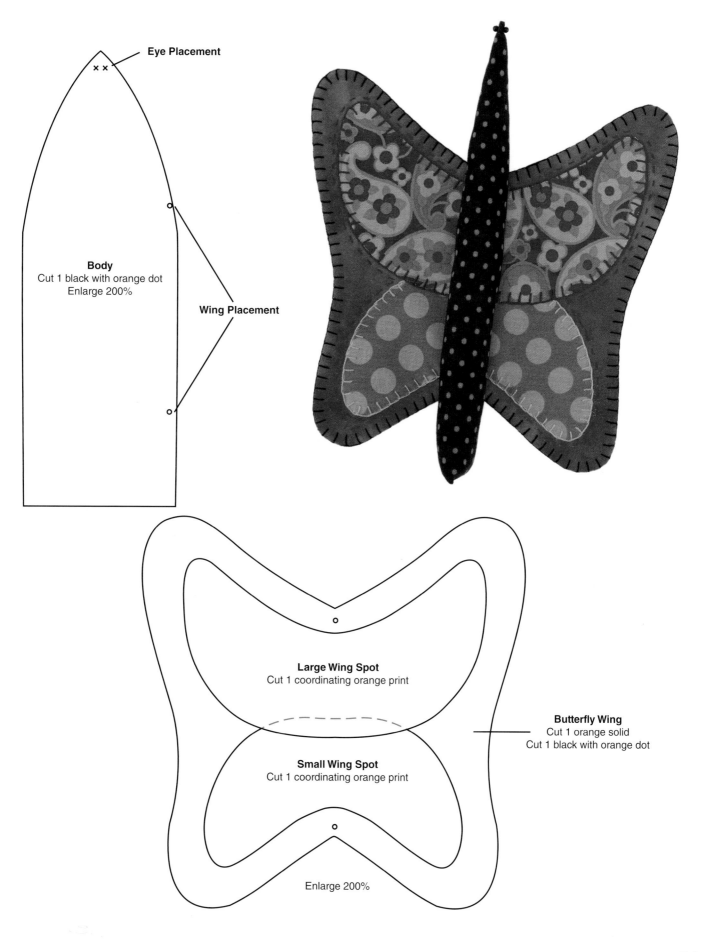

Eye Placement

Body
Cut 1 black with orange dot
Enlarge 200%

Wing Placement

Large Wing Spot
Cut 1 coordinating orange print

Butterfly Wing
Cut 1 orange solid
Cut 1 black with orange dot

Small Wing Spot
Cut 1 coordinating orange print

Enlarge 200%

Fruit Quartet Pot Holders

These pot holders are the perfect blend of beauty and practicality. They make an excellent gift for a hostess or a housewarming.

DESIGN BY MARIAN SHENK

PROJECT SPECIFICATIONS

Skill Level: Beginner
Pot Holder Size: 9¼" x 9¼" each

Fruit Potholder
9¼" x 9¼"
Make 4

MATERIALS

- Variety red, yellow, purple, green and brown scraps
- ¼ yard cream print
- ¼ yard multicolored print
- ⅜ yard solid purple
- ⅜ yard heat-resistant batting
- 3 (1") coordinating buttons
- ¼ yard paper-backed fusible web
- Black and brown fine-line permanent fabric markers
- Cosmetic blush and cotton swabs
- All-purpose threads to match fabrics
- White quilting thread
- Basic sewing tools and supplies

Cutting

1. Cut four 6¾" A squares from cream print.

2. Cut eight 2" x 6¾" C strips and eight 2" x 9¾" B strips from multicolored print.

3. Using Tab pattern on page 26, cut 8 Tab pieces from multicolored print.

4. Cut four 9¾" E squares from solid purple.

5. Cut four 9¾" squares and four Tab pieces from heat-resistant batting.

Completing the Appliqué

1. Prepare appliqué templates using patterns given.

2. Trace appliqué templates on paper side of fusible web, leaving ½" between, for number to cut as directed on patterns. Cut out, leaving approximately ¼" margin around each.

3. Follow manufacturer's instructions and fuse appliqué pieces to fabric scraps as indicated on patterns. Cut out on traced lines.

4. Arrange appliqué pieces on A squares, referring to the Placement Diagram for position, and fuse in place.

5. Machine-stitch around each piece using matching thread and a narrow zigzag or buttonhole stitch.

Completing the Pot Holders

1. Sew C strips to two opposite sides of each square (Figure 1). Sew B strips to top and bottom of each square (Figure 2).

Figure 1

Figure 2

2. Layer an E square right side up, an appliquéd A square facedown and a 9¾" heat-resistant batting square shiny side up and pin along edges.

4. Layer two Tab fabric pieces, right sides together, on one Tab batting piece. Sew around edges, leaving the bottom open. Turn right side out and press. Repeat to make four Tabs.

5. Position a Tab at center of Pot Holder top. Sew around block through all thicknesses, leaving a 2" opening on one side as shown in Figure 3.

Figure 3

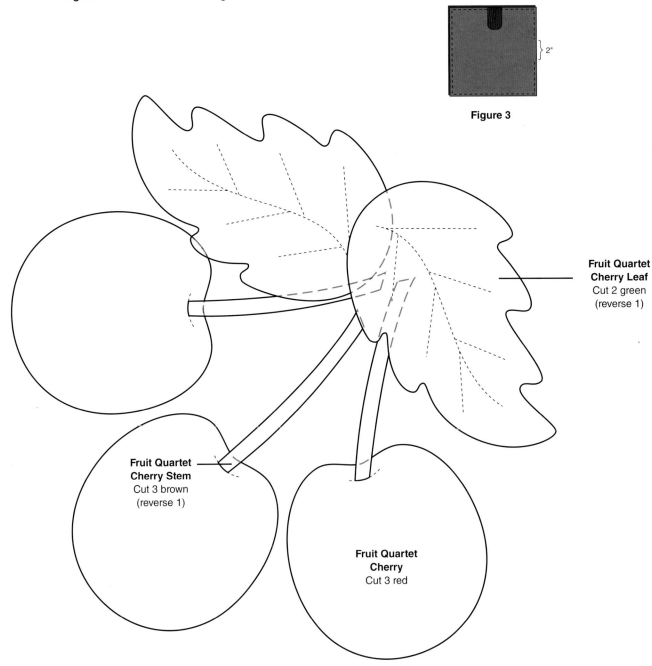

Fruit Quartet Cherry Leaf
Cut 2 green
(reverse 1)

Fruit Quartet Cherry Stem
Cut 3 brown
(reverse 1)

Fruit Quartet Cherry
Cut 3 red

6. Turn right side out and press. Repeat to make four pot holders.

7. Work a 1" buttonhole in each Tab (Figure 4a). Sew buttons at center of lower border of three pot holders referring to Figure 4b.

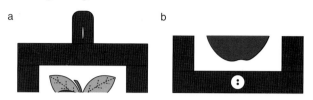

a   b

Figure 4

8. With black and brown markers, fill in details of grapes and leaves as shown on appliqué patterns. Brush pears with cotton swab and cosmetic blush.

9. Machine-quilt around fruit and leaves and in the ditch of borders with quilting thread.

10. Button pot holders together and hang on kitchen wall, ready for use. ■

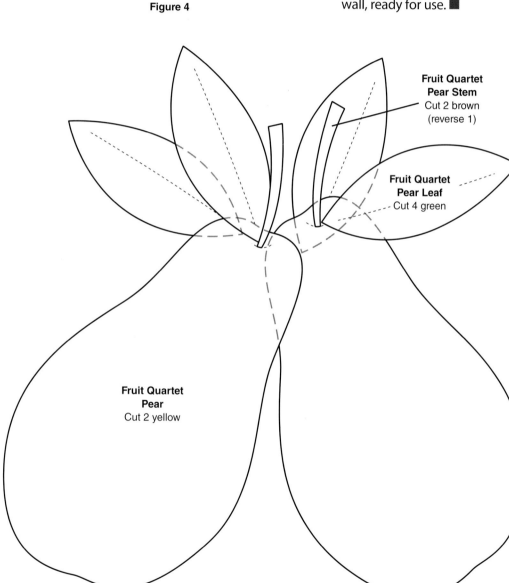

**Fruit Quartet
Pear Stem**
Cut 2 brown
(reverse 1)

**Fruit Quartet
Pear Leaf**
Cut 4 green

**Fruit Quartet
Pear**
Cut 2 yellow

Fruit Quartet Pot Holders
Placement Diagram
9¹⁄₄" x 9¹⁄₄" each

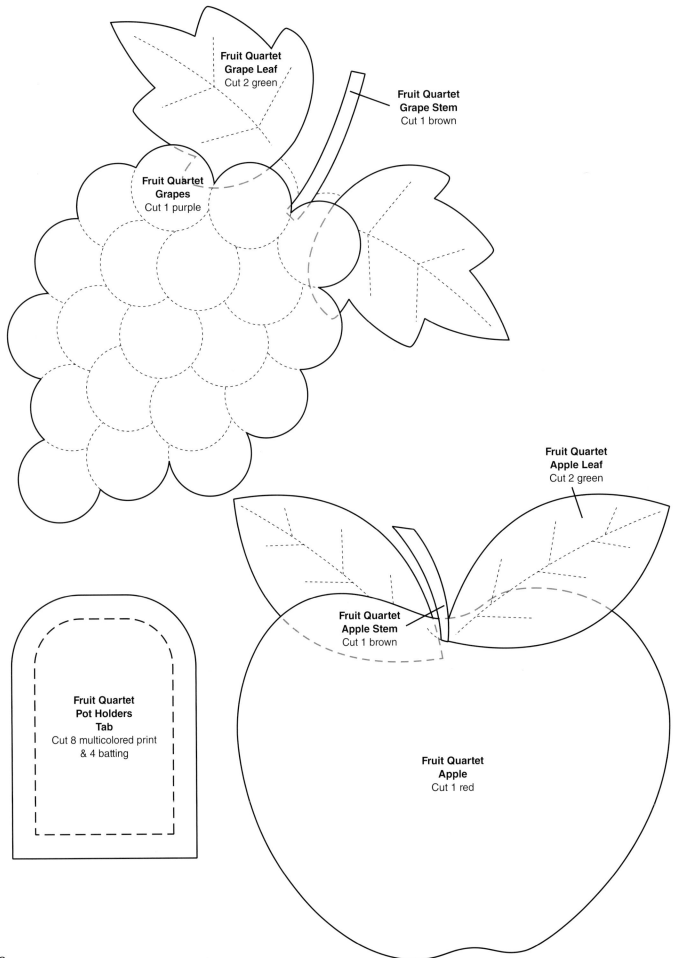

Fruit Quartet Grape Leaf
Cut 2 green

Fruit Quartet Grape Stem
Cut 1 brown

Fruit Quartet Grapes
Cut 1 purple

Fruit Quartet Apple Leaf
Cut 2 green

Fruit Quartet Apple Stem
Cut 1 brown

Fruit Quartet Pot Holders Tab
Cut 8 multicolored print & 4 batting

Fruit Quartet Apple
Cut 1 red

Sassy Slide

Stitch a one-of-a-kind laptop case for your favorite teen. Instructions for adjusting size to fit any computer are included.

DESIGNED & QUILTED BY KAREN BLOCHER

PROJECT SPECIFICATIONS

Skill Level: Beginner
Project Size: Size varies

MATERIALS

- 14–20 (1½" by fabric width) coordinating fabric strips
- ¼ yard coordinating print
- ½ yard coordinating lining
- ½ yard batting
- Neutral-color all-purpose thread
- Quilting thread
- 1½" length hook-and-loop tape
- Machine walking foot (optional)
- Basic sewing tools and supplies

Determining Size of the Laptop Slide

1. Measure the length, width and depth of your laptop. Note these measurements.

2. Add the width measurement of your laptop plus the depth measurement, plus 1" for seam allowances, to determine the width of your slide.

3. Multiply the length of your laptop by 2 and add the depth measurement, plus 1" for seam allowances, to determine the length of your slide. See example in sidebar on page 28.

Completing the Laptop Cover

1. Arrange and join the 1½"-wide strips in a pleasing pattern; join the number of strips needed to create a pieced panel equal to the calculated width of your laptop slide. *Note: Divide the width measurement in half and measure this amount from the center to each outside edge of the panel to evenly distribute strips on both sides of the center as shown in Figure 1.*

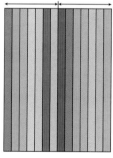

Figure 1

2. Trim the pieced panel created in step 1 to the calculated length of your laptop slide.

3. Cut a strip 5½" by the calculated width of your laptop minus 1" for the flap, using the coordinating print fabric and a cup or plate to create rounded edges on one long side of the flap as shown in Figure 2.

Figure 2

4. Fold and crease the trimmed flap to find the center.

5. Center and sew the flap to one end of the pieced panel to complete the outside panel as shown in Figure 3; press seam toward the flap. *Note: The flap will be slightly narrower than the pieced panel.*

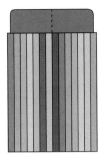

Figure 3

6. Lay the batting flat on a table; place the lining fabric right side up on top of the batting. Place the outside panel right sides together with the lining and pin through all layers.

7. Trim batting and lining edges even with the outside panel.

8. Stitch a ¼" seam all around the edges, leaving a 4" opening on one side; trim batting close to stitching.

9. Turn right side out; press edges flat.

10. Turn the opening edges ¼" to the inside and hand- or machine-stitch opening closed.

11. Quilt as desired by hand or machine. Topstitch ¼" from the edge of the flap.

12. Fold the pieced panel section of the quilted cover in half with right sides together, matching side edges as shown in Figure 4; stitch side edges through all layers. *Note: This seam will be bulky; using a walking foot is suggested.*

Figure 4

13. Finger-press the seams open at the bottom of the cover and flatten the seam against the bag as shown in Figure 5.

Figure 5

14. Measure in from the point half the distance of the depth of your laptop and stitch a straight line perpendicular to the bottom seams to create a square bottom for your cover, again referring to Figure 5.

Determine Size Example

Here is an example of how to determine the size of the pieces to cut for your laptop slide.

1. My laptop measures 11½" (width) x 9½" (length) x 1½" (depth).

2. The width of my laptop slide is: 11½" (width) + 1½" (depth) + 1" (seams) = 14".

3. The length of my laptop slide is: 9½" (top length) + 9½" (bottom length) + 1½" (depth) + 1" (seams) = 21½".

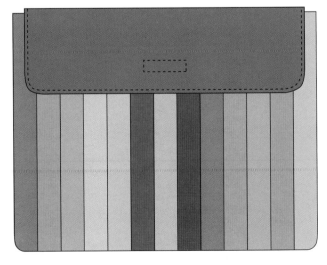

Sassy Slide
Placement Diagram Size Varies

15. Turn the cover right side out and press flat.

16. Center and stitch the piece of loop tape ⅜" from the edge on the inside of the flap as shown in Figure 6.

Figure 6

17. Place your laptop inside the cover and fold the flap down. Mark the area under the loop tape.

18. Remove the laptop. Center and stitch the hook tape on the bag front as marked to complete the laptop slide. ◼

Christmas Card Holder

Whether you use actual handkerchiefs or a preprint handkerchief panel, this card holder is a quick-to-stitch project.

DESIGN BY SANDRA L. HATCH

PROJECT SPECIFICATIONS

Skill Level: Beginner
Card Holder Size: 17" x 29"

MATERIALS

- 3 (10½") handkerchiefs or preprinted handkerchief squares
- ⅝ yard dark green print
- ⅝ yard red snowflake print
- Backing 23" x 35"
- 1 package craft-size batting (34" x 45")
- All-purpose thread to match fabrics
- Quilting thread
- Quilt basting spray
- Basic sewing tools and supplies

Cutting

1. Cut one 13½" by fabric width strip from dark green print. Subcut strip into one 11½" x 13½" C and two 8½" x 13½" D rectangles and one 2½" x 13½" E strip.

2. Cut two 2½" by fabric width strips from dark green print. Subcut into two 2½" by 28½" F strips.

3. Cut one 7⅞" by width of fabric from red snowflake print; subcut into three 7⅞" squares and one 4" x 16" rectangle. Cut squares in half on one diagonal to make six B triangles.

4. Cut three 2¼" by fabric width strips from red snowflake print for binding.

5. Cut three 9" x 15" and one 23" x 35" rectangles from batting.

Completing the Holder

1. Fold each A handkerchief on the diagonal and crease.

2. Open, center and fold each A handkerchief over one 15" edge of the 15" x 9" batting rectangles as shown in Figure 1; pin and baste to hold in place.

Figure 1

3. Pin the diagonal edge of a B triangle right sides together on one diagonal edge of one layered A; stitch as shown in Figure 2. Press B to the right side.

Figure 2

4. Repeat step 3 with a second B on the opposite raw edge of A to complete an A-B pocket unit as shown in Figure 3. Repeat to make three A-B pocket units.

Figure 3

5. Trim each A-B pocket unit to 13½" x 7".

6. Lay the 23" x 35" batting piece on a flat surface. Lay the C piece 2" down from the top of the batting and centered from side to side as shown in Figure 4.

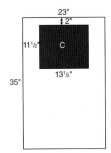

Figure 4

7. Lay one A-B pocket unit right side up on top of C, aligning side and bottom edges as shown in Figure 5; machine-baste edges in place through all layers.

Figure 5

8. Place D right sides together with the basted unit, aligning 13½" edge of D with the bottom of the A-B pocket unit as shown in Figure 6; stitch through all layers. Press D to the right side.

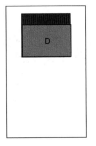

Figure 6

9. Repeat step 7 with another A-B pocket unit on D as shown in Figure 7.

Figure 7

10. Repeat steps 8 and 9 to add a second D piece and another A-B pocket unit as shown in Figure 8.

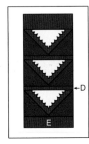

Figure 8

11. Repeat step 8 with E to complete the center section, again referring to Figure 8.

12. Stitch F strips to opposite long sides to complete the pieced top; press seams toward F strips.

13. Place backing piece wrong sides together with the batting side of the stitched unit; spray-baste to hold layers together.

14. Stitch in the ditch of seams of E and F pieces and along ditch of seams between A-B pocket units and the background to hold layers together.

15. Trim batting and backing edges even with the stitched unit.

16. Fold the short ends of the 4" x 16" sleeve strip ¼" to the wrong side; press and stitch to hem.

17. Fold the strip in half with wrong sides together along length and machine-baste to make a tube; press flat.

18. Align the basted raw edges even with the top raw edge of the backing piece as shown in Figure 9; baste to hold in place.

Figure 9

19. Join binding strips on short ends with diagonal seams to make one long strip; trim seams to ¼" and press seams open.

20. Fold the binding strip in half with wrong sides together along length; press.

21. Sew binding to quilt edges, matching raw edges, mitering corners and overlapping ends.

22. Fold binding to the back side and stitch in place to finish.

23. Hand-stitch folded bottom edge of sleeve strip in place on the backing side to finish. ■

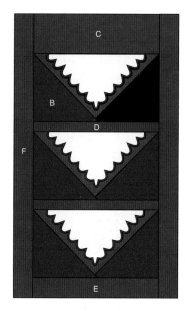

Christmas Card Holder
Placement Diagram 17" x 29"

Quick Mug Rugs

In an hour or two, these mug rugs will be ready to use. Flannel fabric and raggedy edges make them super easy. Tie a set of four together with a ribbon for the perfect secret-pal gift.

DESIGN BY CAROLYN S. VAGTS

PROJECT SPECIFICATIONS

Skill Level: Beginner
Mug Rug Size: 6" x 6"

MATERIALS

- 12 (6") squares assorted flannel scraps or ½ yard total flannel scraps
- 6 (5") squares batting scraps or ¼ yard batting
- All-purpose thread to match fabric
- Basic sewing tools and supplies

Cutting

1. If using individual scraps, trim flannel scraps to 6" square, making 12 fabric squares and six 5" batting squares.

2. If using yardage, cut two 6" by fabric width strips flannel; subcut strips into (12) 6" squares flannel.

3. Cut one 5" by batting width strip; subcut into six 5" squares of batting.

Completing the Mug Rugs

1. Layer a 6" flannel square right side down with a 5" batting square centered on top and a second 6" flannel square right side up (Figure 1). Pin to hold.

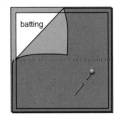

Figure 1

2. Stitch on both diagonals, making an X and referring to Figure 2.

 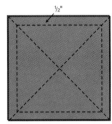

Figure 2   **Figure 3**

3. Stitch ½" from all four sides (Figure 3).

4. Using a small pair of scissors, snip around all four sides about ½" apart, referring to Figure 4 and making sure not to clip seam.

5. Repeat steps 1–4 to make 12 mug rugs.

Figure 4

6. Wash mug rugs several times to fray the cut edges and give them a chenille look. ■

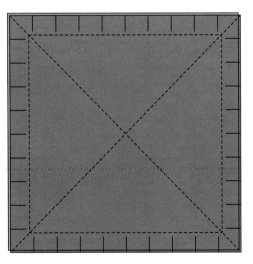

Quick Mug Rugs
Placement Diagram 6" x 6"

Strip-Pieced Place Mats

These quick-to-stitch place mats can be started this afternoon
and will be ready to use by dinnertime.

DESIGN BY CONNIE KAUFFMAN

PROJECT NOTE

Materials listed and instructions make one placemat.
Increase materials by number of placemats
being made.

PROJECT SPECIFICATIONS

Skill Level: Beginner
Place Mat: 17" x 12"

MATERIALS

- ⅛ yard coordinating print 1
- ⅛ yard coordinating print 2
- ½ yard large print
- Batting 12½" x 17½"
- All-purpose thread to match fabrics
- Basic sewing tools and supplies

Cutting

1. Cut one 1" by fabric width strip from print 1; subcut
into two 1" x 12½" B strips.

2. Cut one 1" x fabric width strip from print 2; subcut
into four 1" x 12½" B strips.

3. Cut one 12½" by fabric width rectangle from large
print. Subcut into one 12½" x 17½" backing rectangle
and seven 2½" x 12½" A strips.

Completing a Place Mat

1. Arrange the A strips in the order cut from fabric;
place the B strips between the A strips in a pleasing
arrangement. Join the strips along the 12½" sides;
press seams toward A.

All-Occasion Variations

*Make a table runner to match your Strip-Pieced Place
Mats with just a few extra strips. Because the main print
in the runner is larger and busier than in the place mat,
wider A and B strips were used to make the division more
obvious. This is an easy remedy to use, even for the
place mat.*

*Start looking for the perfect large print to make your own
table set. But be careful, this pattern can be addictive!*

2. Place batting piece on a flat surface; lay the backing piece right side up on batting. Place the pieced top right side down on backing; baste layers together.

3. Stitch around outside edges, leaving a 3" opening on one side for turning.

4. Trim corners; trim batting close to seam.

5. Turn right side out through opening; press edges flat.

6. Press opening edges ¼" to the inside; hand-stitch opening closed.

7. Stitch in the ditch of all seams and hide thread endings to finish. ■

Strip-Pieced Place Mats
Placement Diagram 17" x 12"

Mini Dresden Ornament

Use English paper-piecing techniques to create the wreath on this Christmas ornament. A ribbon bow provides the hanger.

DESIGN BY CHRIS MALONE

PROJECT NOTE

Materials listed are for one Mini Dresden Ornament. To make more than one, increase the amount of materials by number of ornaments to be made.

PROJECT SPECIFICATIONS

Skill Level: Confident Beginner
Ornament Size: 4½" x 4½"

MATERIALS

- 2 (5") squares red or green Christmas print for ornament front and back
- 1 (5") square contrasting Christmas print for Dresden Plate appliqué
- Batting 5" square
- 1 sheet 8½" x 11" copy paper
- ½ yard red ⅝"-wide wire-edge ribbon
- Fiberfill stuffing or 1 cup Christmas scented potpourri
- All-purpose thread to match fabrics
- Ecru hand-quilting thread
- Basic sewing tools and supplies

Completing Dresden Plate Appliqué

1. Trace the dresden plate pattern given on page 40 eight times onto copy paper and carefully cut out on traced lines.

2. Pin each paper pattern to the wrong side of the appliqué fabric, leaving ½" between pieces. Cut out pieces ¼" away from the pattern edges (Figure 1).

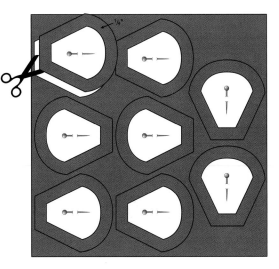

Figure 1

3. Fold and finger-press the fabric over the paper pattern's edges; hand-baste through the paper and fabric as shown in Figure 2. Repeat with all eight pieces.

Figure 2

4. Position two pieces right sides together and sew along straight edge with small whipstitches, catching fabric but not paper as shown in Figure 3.

Figure 3

5. Repeat step 4, adding pieces until a circle of shapes is completed to make the dresden plate wreath appliqué (Figure 4). Lightly press flat. Remove basting stitches and paper pieces from appliqué. Paper patterns can be reused.

Figure 4

Completing the Ornament

1. Center, pin and hand-appliqué dresden plate wreath on ornament front square, using small invisible stitches and matching thread, sewing around all curved edges.

2. Baste a batting square to wrong side of appliquéd front. Hand-quilt ³⁄₁₆" from the outer edge of the wreath using a long stitch.

3. Pin appliquéd front and back squares right sides together, edges matching, and sew around, leaving a 2" opening on one side.

4. Trim corners and cut batting close to stitching line. Turn right side out.

5. Stuff firmly with fiberfill or Christmas-scented potpourri. Fold opening seam allowance to inside and stitch opening closed.

6. Fold ribbon in half and sew gathering stitches through both layers 4" down from top of loop to make hanging loop. Pull thread to gather and knot thread but do not clip.

7. Tie a bow directly below the gathering stitches. Use gathering thread to tack bow to top of ornament as shown in Placement Diagram. Tie knot at each end of ribbon tails to complete. ■

Mini Dresden Wreath Ornament
Placement Diagram 4¹⁄₂" x 4¹⁄₂"

Dresden Plate Pattern
Cut 8 from paper

10-Hour Treats

Imagine giving someone you love a handmade Ruffled Rose Pillow or Simply Scrappy Place Mats that you quilted in just a weekend. They will be thrilled with their beautiful gift and you will have the satisfaction of knowing you created a gift that will be cherished for a lifetime. With a wide range of projects from home decor to totes, you may find it hard to part with these fun and quick 10-hour projects.

Ruffled Rose Pillow

Stitch this decorative pillow embellished with fabric roses and delight the loved one in your life.

DESIGN BY CHRIS MALONE

PROJECT SPECIFICATIONS

Skill Level: Confident Beginner
Pillow Size: 16" x 16"

MATERIALS

- Scraps of white, light ivory and light tan prints or tonals at least 5" square
- 1 fat quarter each 2 light green prints or tonals
- ¼ yard each 3 medium-to-dark rose prints or tonals
- ⅓ yard light rose print or tonal
- ½ yard light neutral print or tonal
- Scrap low-loft batting or fleece
- Batting 16½" x 16½"
- 1 (16" x 16") pillow form
- Scrap stiff interfacing
- 3 (⅝") white shank buttons
- Size 12 pink pearl cotton
- Fabric basting spray (optional)
- Template material
- All-purpose thread to match fabrics
- Basic sewing tools and supplies

Cutting

1. Cut a total of (16) 2½" A squares from white, light ivory and light tan prints or tonals.

2. Cut a total of (12) 4½" B squares from white, light ivory and light tan prints or tonals.

3. Cut one 12½" by fabric width strip light neutral print or tonal; subcut strip into two 16½" C rectangles.

4. Cut one 5" by fabric width D strip from each medium-to-dark rose print or tonal.

5. Cut two 4" by fabric width strips light rose print or tonal; subcut strips into three 21" E strips.

6. Cut three 2"-diameter circles from stiff interfacing for flower bases.

Completing the Pillow

1. Arrange the 16 A squares into four groups of four different squares. Select a group and join two squares from the group to make a row referring to Figure 1; press seam to the right. Repeat with remaining two squares to make a second row; press seam to the left.

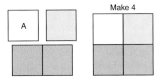

Figure 1

2. Join rows to make a 4½" Four-Patch square, again referring to Figure 1. Repeat with remaining groups of A squares to make four Four-Patch squares.

3. Arrange the Four-Patch squares with B squares, as shown in Figure 2, to make four rows of four blocks each.

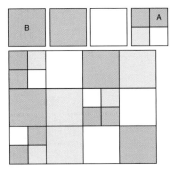

Figure 2

4. Join squares in rows, pressing seams in opposite directions for each row.

5. Join rows, again referring to Figure 2; press seams in one direction to complete pieced pillow top.

6. Center pieced pillow top on the 16½" square of batting and baste together with thread, pins or fabric basting spray. Quilt as desired.

7. Fold and press ¼" to wrong side of one 16½" edge of one C rectangle (Figure 3).

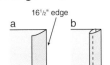

Figure 3

8. Repeat step 7, folding and pressing again ¼" to wrong side. Edgestitch along first fold to make a double-turned hem on C, again referring to Figure 3. Repeat steps 7 and 8 on a second C rectangle.

9. Pin C rectangles to pieced pillow top, overlapping hemmed edges of C and matching raw edges to pieced pillow top as shown in Figure 4.

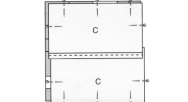

Figure 4

10. Sew around all edges using a ¼" seam allowance. Trim corners and turn right side out.

Completing the Ruffled Roses

1. To make leaves, prepare leaf template by tracing leaf pattern onto template material, transferring all pattern markings to template.

2. Trace three leaves, ½" apart, onto wrong side of one light green print or tonal and two leaves, ½" apart, on second light green print or tonal.

3. Fold fabric in half right sides together and pin to low-loft batting or fleece.

4. Sew around each leaf on traced line, leaving straight bottom edge open. Cut out ⅛" away from stitching. Trim leaf points and batting/fleece close to stitching. Turn right sides out and press flat.

5. Turn straight bottom edge ¼" to inside and press; stitch along bottom edge to close opening. Transfer vein lines to each leaf; stitch on the marked vein lines twice to complete leaves as shown in Figure 5.

Figure 5

6. Fold and baste pleat in bottom edge referring to Figure 6 to complete leaves. Set aside.

Figure 6

7. To make ruffled roses, fold D right sides together along length; join on short ends. Trim corners and turn right side out; press flat.

8. Stitch over pearl cotton, positioned ¼" from raw edges, with a wide zigzag stitch to make a gathering thread (Figure 7). Do not catch pearl cotton in stitching.

Figure 7

9. Knot pearl cotton and zigzag threads at one end to secure. Pull pearl cotton to gather D into a ruffle approximately half the original length. Loosely tie thread ends.

10. Repeat steps 7–9 with each D and E strip.

11. Take one D ruffle and form a flat circle with a ½" center opening and two or three layers of ruffles as shown in Figure 8. Adjust gathering as necessary and tightly tie thread ends to secure; pin layers together to make a flower. Repeat with all D ruffle strips.

Figure 8

12. Center D ruffled layers on an interfacing circle. Using a double thread, hand-tack layers to circle around center opening in several places to hold.

13. Roll an E ruffle into a soft cone and hand-tack to secure (Figure 9). Knot thread but do not clip it. Bring needle up through flower center and a button, going back down through center.

Figure 9

14. Using same thread, attach button and flower center to interfacing circle and D ruffled layers.

15. Repeat steps 11–14 to make three ruffled roses.

Attaching the Embellishments

1. Insert the base of a leaf between the flower and interfacing; whipstitch in place to interfacing.

2. Add three leaves to one flower and one each to the remaining two flowers.

3. Arrange the flowers in a corner of the pieced pillow top as shown in Placement Diagram and photo. Attach by hand using doubled thread and whipstitching interfacing to pillow to complete.

4. Insert pillow form through back opening to complete the pillow. ■

Ruffled Rose Pillow
Placement Diagram 16" x 16"

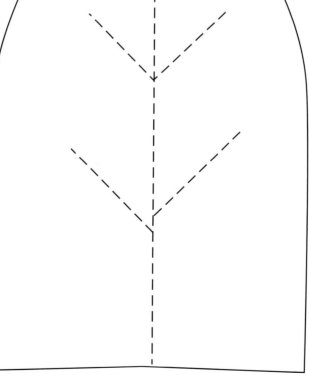

Leaf
Cut per instructions

Chair Chatelaine

You'll love keeping everything near at hand when you're quilting, but you may find someone else borrowing your chatelaine to hold their glasses and perhaps a remote or two.

DESIGN BY KATE LAUCOMER

PROJECT SPECIFICATIONS

Skill Level: Beginner
Chatelaine Size: 5½" x 22"
Block Size: 5" x 6½"
Number of Blocks: 2

Flower
5" x 6½" Block
Make 2

MATERIALS

- Scraps 3 different pinks for paper-pieced flowers
- Scraps green for paper-pieced leaves
- ¾ yard blue print
- 2 squares batting 6½" x 6½"
- Batting 11" x 28"
- Neutral-color all-purpose thread
- Light and dark blue quilting thread
- Thin paper
- Basic sewing tools and supplies

Cutting

1. Cut one 11" by fabric width strip blue print; subcut strip into one 28" backing piece and two 5½" x 6½" rectangles for block/pocket backings.

2. Cut one 5½" x 22" A rectangle blue print.

3. Cut two 2¼" by fabric width strips blue print for binding.

Completing the Blocks

1. Prepare three copies of the flower paper-piecing pattern. Cut out one pattern on the marked lines to make templates for each shape; trace shapes right side up onto the wrong side of fabrics as directed on each piece for color, leaving ½" between shapes.

2. Cut out shapes, leaving at least ¼" beyond the traced lines as shown in Figure 1.

Figure 1

3. Select one paper foundation and piece 1; turn paper to the unmarked side and pin piece 1 on the space marked 1 on the opposite side. Select piece 2 and pin right sides together with piece 1 on the side with the line between pieces 1 and 2 as shown in Figure 2.

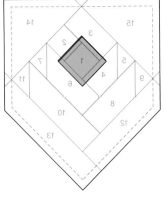

Figure 2

4. Turn the paper over and stitch on the line between pieces 1 and 2, taking at least one stitch before the beginning of the line and at the end as shown in Figure 3.

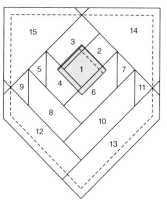

Figure 3

5. Turn the paper over; press piece 2 to the right side as shown in Figure 4.

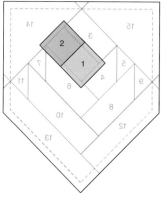

Figure 4

6. Repeat steps 3–5 with piece 3 on pieces 1 and 2 as shown in Figure 5.

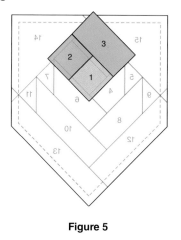

Figure 5

7. Repeat steps 3–5 with all pieces; trim outer edges even with outer line on paper pattern to complete one Flower block. Remove paper backing.

8. Repeat steps 3–7 to complete a second Flower block.

Completing the Chatelaine

1. Layer a 6½" x 6½" batting square with one 6½" x 6½" backing square right side up and a Flower block right side down. Sew across the 5½" straight edge on the block as shown in Figure 6.

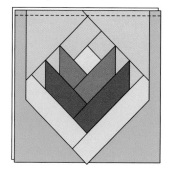

Figure 6

2. Flip the Flower block to the right side, sandwiching the batting between the backing and the block as shown in Figure 7; press.

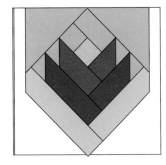

Figure 7

3. Quilt in the ditch of the seams of the Flower block by hand or machine.

4. When quilting is complete, trim the batting and backing squares even with the edges of the Flower block as shown in Figure 8.

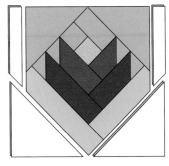

Figure 8

5. Mark a 1⅝" diagonal grid on the A rectangle as shown in Figure 9.

Figure 9

6. Sandwich the 11" x 28" backing piece between the marked A strip and the 11" x 28" backing piece. Quilt on marked lines by hand or machine.

7. When quilting is complete, trim backing and batting edges even with A.

8. Layer the quilted Flower block right side up at each end of A and trim the quilted A ends at angles to match the Flower block as shown in Figure 10.

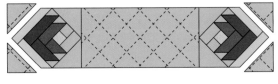

Figure 10

9. Machine-baste the outer edges of the Flower block to A as shown in Figure 11.

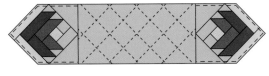

Figure 11

10. Join binding strips on short ends with diagonal seams as shown in Figure 12; press seams open.

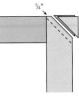

Figure 12

11. Fold the binding strip in half with wrong sides together along length and press.

12. Stitch the binding to the chatelaine, matching raw edges of binding to the raw edges of the chatelaine, mitering corners and overlapping at the beginning and end.

13. Turn the binding to the wrong side and hand-stitch in place to finish. ■

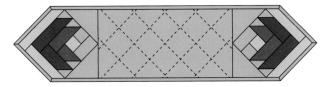

Chair Chatelaine
Placement Diagram 5½" x 22"

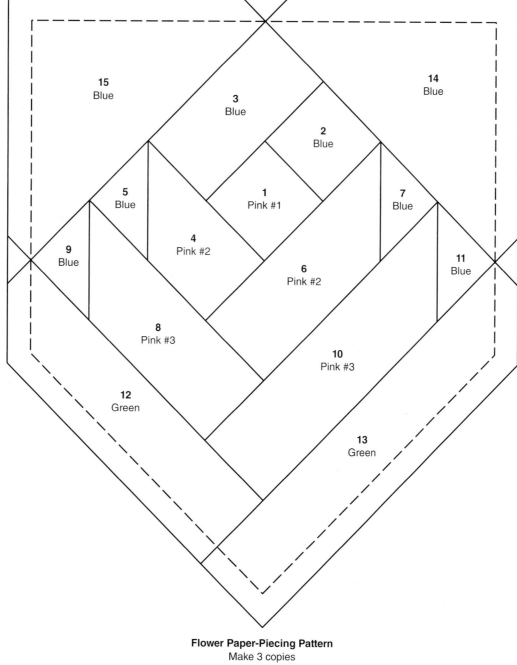

15 Blue	3 Blue		14 Blue
		2 Blue	
5 Blue		1 Pink #1	7 Blue
9 Blue	4 Pink #2		11 Blue
		6 Pink #2	
	8 Pink #3		
12 Green		10 Pink #3	
	13 Green		

Flower Paper-Piecing Pattern
Make 3 copies

Simply Scrappy Place Mats

Here's a great project for using all the tiny scraps you couldn't bear to throw away!

DESIGN BY LUCY FAZELY

PROJECT SPECIFICATIONS

Skill Level: Beginner
Place Mat Size: 12" x 18"

PROJECT NOTE

Materials listed and instructions are for two place mats.

MATERIALS

- Variety of 2" square bright print scraps
- ¼ yard coordinating bright print
- ½ yard total white tonal scraps
- ½ yard backing fabric
- Batting: 2 (13" x 19") pieces
- Coordinating general-purpose thread
- White quilting thread
- Basic sewing tools and supplies

Cutting

1. Cut (96) 2" squares from bright print scraps.

2. Cut three 2¼" by fabric width strips from coordinating bright print for binding.

3. Cut (48) 3½" squares from white tonal scraps.

4. Cut one 13" by fabric width strip from backing fabric; subcut into two 13" x 19" backing pieces.

Completing the Place Mats

1. Fold each bright print square in half diagonally and press as shown in Figure 1.

Figure 1

2. Pin two folded triangles on opposite corners of a white tonal square, as shown in Figure 2, to make a triangle unit. Repeat to make 48 triangle units.

Figure 2

3. Sew six triangle units together with units facing in the same direction, referring to Figure 3, to make a row. Repeat to make four rows.

Figure 3

4. Sew rows together, referring to Figure 4, with triangle units facing in same direction.

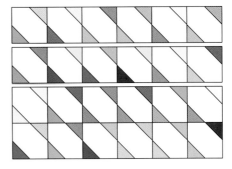

Figure 4

5. An alternate layout is shown in Figure 5 that will create a diamond pattern.

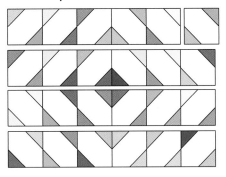

Figure 5

6. Repeat steps 3–5 to make a second place mat.

7. Press place mat tops on both sides; check for proper seam pressing and trim all loose threads.

8. Sandwich batting between the stitched tops and the prepared backing pieces; pin or baste layers together to hold. Quilt on marked lines and as desired by hand or machine.

9. When quilting is complete, remove pins or basting. Trim batting and backing fabric edges even with raw edges of place mat tops.

10. Join binding strips on short ends with diagonal seams to make one long strip; trim seams to ¼" and press seams open.

11. Fold the binding strip in half with wrong sides together along length; press.

12. Sew binding to quilt edges, matching raw edges, mitering corners and overlapping ends.

13. Fold binding to the back side and stitch in place to finish. ■

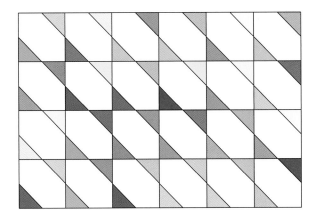

Simple Scrappy Place Mats
Placement Diagram 12" x 18"

Wild Goose Chase Tote

With sturdy construction, quirky design features and lots of pockets, this bag can be used as a tote or oversized purse.

DESIGN BY SANDRA L. HATCH

PROJECT SPECIFICATIONS

Skill Level: Intermediate
Tote Size: 15" x 15" x 4"

MATERIALS

- 1 fat quarter pink with yellow dots
- 1 fat quarter lime green print
- ⅔ yard bright pink print
- 1 yard cream floral print
- 1 yard coordinating-color lining fabric
- ½ yard 45"-wide fusible fleece
- All-purpose thread to match fabrics
- Quilting thread
- 1 (1⅜") coordinating-color button
- 1⅔ yards lime green jumbo rickrack
- 1 sheet plastic canvas
- Basic sewing tools and supplies

Cutting

1. Cut two 3½" x 22" strips pink with yellow dot; subcut strips into (16) 2" A rectangles.

2. Cut three 2" x 22" strips lime green print; subcut strips into (32) 2" B squares.

3. Cut one 10½" by fabric width strip bright pink print. Subcut strip into one 2½" C strip, one 10½" D square and one 15½" E pocket lining rectangle.

4. Cut two 3½" by fabric width strips bright pink print; subcut strips into two 30½" J handle strips.

5. Cut one 9" by fabric width strip bright pink print; subcut strip into one 9" x 15½" K and one 2" x 6½" P.

6. Cut one 19½" by fabric width strip cream floral print. Subcut strip into one 12½" F, one 2½" G, one 17½" H and two 2½" I pieces.

7. Cut one 8½" by fabric width strip cream floral print. Subcut strip into two 15½" M and one 10½" O.

8. Cut one 17½" by fabric width strip lining; subcut strip into two 19½" L.

9. Cut one 4½" by fabric width strip lining; subcut strip into one 15½" N.

10. Cut the following from fusible fleece: one 10½" x 15½" and four 17½" x 19½" rectangles and one ½" x 6½" and two 1" x 30½" strips.

11. Cut two 4½" x 15½" rectangles plastic canvas for bag bottom stiffener.

Completing the Outer Pocket

1. Draw a diagonal line from corner to corner on the wrong side of each B square.

2. Place a marked B square right sides together on one end of A and stitch on the marked line as shown in Figure 1. Trim seam to ¼" and press B to the right side, again referring to Figure 1.

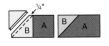

| Figure 1 | Figure 2 |

3. Repeat step 2 on the opposite end of A to complete a Flying Geese unit referring to Figure 2. Repeat to make a total of 16 Flying Geese units. Set aside 10 units for front top band.

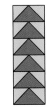

4. Join six Flying Geese units to make a Flying Geese strip as shown in Figure 3. Press seams in one direction.

Figure 3

5. Sew C to the right side edge and D to the left side edge of the Flying Geese strip, matching bottom edges, to make the Flying Geese section as shown in Figure 4. Press seams toward C and D.

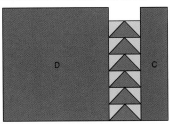

Figure 4

6. Fuse the 10½" x 15½" rectangle fusible fleece to the wrong side of the Flying Geese section.

7. Quilt as desired.

8. Mark a point 3" up from bottom left side of D in Flying Geese section as shown in Figure 5.

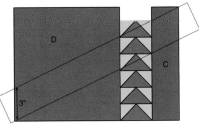

Figure 5

9. Using a ruler and rotary cutter, trim the Flying Geese section from marked point on D to top right-hand corner of C, again referring to Figure 5, to make the outer triangle pocket.

10. Cut a piece of lime green jumbo rickrack the length of diagonal edge of quilted triangle pocket. Baste rickrack to diagonal edge using ¼" seam, stitching along rickrack center as shown in Figure 6.

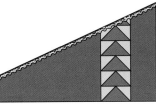

Figure 6

11. With E on bottom, place quilted triangle pocket and E right sides together on flat surface. Trim E even with triangle pocket and pin together.

12. Stitch all around, leaving 4" open on straight bottom edge of triangle pocket. Turn right side out through opening; press edges flat. Turn opening edges to inside along seam allowance and hand-stitch opening closed to line and finish the quilted triangle pocket.

13. Topstitch ¼" from quilted triangle pocket diagonal edge. Set aside.

Completing the Outer Tote

1. Select and join 10 Flying Geese units; adding I rectangles to each end to make a Flying Geese strip (Figure 7). Press seams in one direction.

Figure 7

2. Sew G to top and F to bottom of Flying Geese strip to complete tote front as shown in Figure 8; press seams toward F and G.

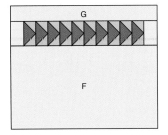

Figure 8

3. Bond a 17½" x 19½" fusible fleece rectangle to the wrong side of the tote front.

4. Quilt tote front as desired.

5. Mark and cut out a 2" square from each bottom corner as shown in Figure 9.

Figure 9

6. Center and pin quilted triangle pocket to outer tote front ½" above trimmed bottom corners as shown in Figure 10. Topstitch pocket sides and bottom ¼" from edges.

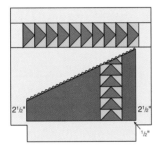

Figure 10

7. Divide the pocket into three pocket sections according to your needs; mark and stitch pocket lines to complete the bag front.

8. Bond the remaining 17½" x 19½" rectangle fusible fleece to wrong side of H.

9. Quilt as desired, then measure and trim bottom corners as in step 5 to make outer tote back.

10. Place front and back pieces right sides together; stitch sides and bottom (Figure 11). Press seams to one side.

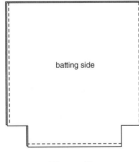

batting side

Figure 11

11. Fold bottom corners, matching seams, and stitch to make a square bottom as shown in Figure 12.

Figure 12

12. Cut a piece of lime green jumbo rickrack the measurement of top edge of bag plus ½".

13. Pin and baste rickrack in place on right side of bag top edge, overlapping ends and referring to step 10 of Completing the Outer Pocket.

Completing the Tote Lining

1. Bond a 17½" x 19½" rectangle fusible fleece to wrong side of each same-size lining rectangle.

2. Quilt rectangles as desired.

3. Cut out 2" squares in each bottom corner referring to Step 5 and Figure 9 of Completing the Outer Tote.

4. Place two M rectangles right sides together. Stitch both short ends and one long side together. Turn right side out; press flat.

5. Fold each short end and one long edge of N strip to wrong side ¼" and press. Stitch the unpressed edge of N to the raw edges of M right sides together (Figure 13).

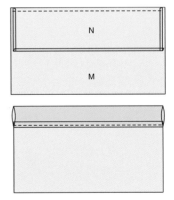

Figure 13

6. Press N up and over raw edges to right side and covering seam. Edgestitch the pressed edge of N in place to complete the M-N pocket, again referring to Figure 13.

7. Center and pin the M-N pocket ½" above the cutout corners referring to step 6 and Figure 10 of Completing the Outer Tote for positioning. Stitch in place, leaving top edge open. Divide the pocket into three sections and stitch to complete pocket.

8. Fold O in half right sides together to make a 5½" x 8½" pocket. Stitch sides and bottom together, leaving 3" opening on one side. Turn right side out through opening; press flat. Press opening edges to inside and hand-stitch opening closed.

9. Center and pin O pocket 3½" down from top of remaining tote lining piece. Stitch sides and bottom of pocket in place to complete.

10. Place the two tote lining pieces right sides together and stitch sides and bottom, leaving 6" opening in bottom seam. Press seams flat.

11. Stitch bottom corners referring to step 11 of Completing the Outer Tote to complete the bag lining.

Completing the Tote

1. Center and bond a 1"-wide strip of fusible fleece to the center of each J handle strip.

2. Fold one edge of the J strip over the fleece and press. Fold ¼" to wrong side of remaining edge then fold over fleece and press.

3. Stitch folded edge in place; topstitch ¼" from each edge to complete tote handle. Repeat steps 2 and 3 to make a second handle.

4. Pin and machine-baste ends of handle strips 5" in from each side seam on the top front and back of outer tote as shown in Figure 14.

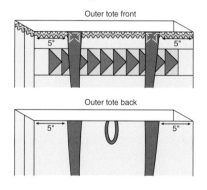

Figure 14

5. Repeat steps 2 and 3 with P except stitch close to edges. Center and machine-baste P to outer back top edge making button loop, again referring to Figure 14.

6. Turn the outer tote wrong side out; insert bag lining right sides together, matching side seams. Stitch around top edge.

7. Turn tote right side out through opening in lining. Hand-stitch lining opening closed.

8. Push lining to bag inside; press top edge and topstitch ¼" from top edge.

9. Center and sew the button 1¾" from top edge of outer tote front.

10. Fold and press ¼" to wrong side of each 8½" end of K. Fold again ¼" to wrong side and stitch to hem ends. Fold K right sides together along length and stitch to make a tube. Turn right side out and press with seam on one side.

11. Insert the two 4" x 15½" plastic canvas rectangles inside the K tube; place in bottom of tote to finish. ▗

Wild Goose Chase Tote
Placement Diagram 15" x 15" x 4"

Wild Goose Chase Wallet

Find your favorite scraps and turn them into what will become your favorite travel wallet. There is a place for everything—travel papers, IDs, money and lipstick too!

DESIGN BY SANDRA L. HATCH

PROJECT SPECIFICATIONS

Skill Level: Advanced
Size: 9" x 4½" folded; 9" x 13½" open flat

MATERIALS

- ⅜ yard bright pink floral
- ½ yard lime green print
- ½ yard pink with yellow dots
- ½ yard 22"-wide fusible fleece
- All-purpose thread to match fabrics
- Quilting thread
- ⅝ yard 18"-wide lightweight fusible interfacing
- ½ yard ¾"-wide hook-and-loop tape
- 2 (½") D rings
- 2 (1½") swivel snap hooks
- Scrap clear vinyl, at least 3" x 4"
- Fabric glue
- Denim/Jeans machine needles (size 14–18)
- Basic sewing tools and supplies

Cutting

1. Cut one 9½" by fabric width strip pink with yellow dots. Subcut strip into one each of the following: 9½" x 13½" D, 3½" x 9½" E, 4½" x 9½" F, 5½" x 9½" G, 6½" x 9½" H and 9½" N square.

2. Cut one 3½" by fabric width strip pink with yellow dots. Subcut strip into three 3½" x 2" A rectangles and two 3½" x 4½" C rectangles.

3. Cut one 9½" by fabric width strip bright pink floral. Subcut the strip into the following: one 9½" O square, one 9½" x 13½" J, two 1½" x 9½" M strips, one 2¾" x 3½" L and one 2¾" x 6½" K.

4. Cut one 2" by fabric width strip lime green print; subcut strip into six 2" B squares. Trim remainder of strip to 1½" and subcut into two 1½" x 3½" P strips, one 1½" x 2¾" Q binding strip and one 2¼" x 9½" R binding strip.

5. Cut two 1½" by fabric width lime green print for S handle strips.

6. From remainder of lime green print, cut enough 2¼" wide bias strips to total 40" when joined.

7. Cut one 3" x 9½" and two 9½" x 17½" fusible fleece rectangles.

8. Cut ½" strips fusible fleece to total 61" in length. Subcut two 3½" lengths for P strips and use remaining 54" for S handle strips.

9. Cut two 9½" squares lightweight fusible interfacing.

10. Trim vinyl scrap to 2¾" x 3¾".

11. Cut one 4" length and one 8¼" length of ¾"-wide hook-and-loop tape.

Completing the Outer Wallet

1. Draw a diagonal line from corner to corner on the wrong side of each B square.

2. Place a B square right sides together on one end of an A rectangle. Stitch on the marked line as shown in Figure 1. Trim seam to ¼" and press B to right side, again referring to Figure 1.

Figure 1

3. Repeat step 2 on opposite end of A to complete a Flying Geese unit referring to Figure 2; repeat to make a total of three Flying Geese units.

Flying geese unit
Make 3

Figure 2

4. Join the three Flying Geese units to make a Flying Geese strip as shown in Figure 3; press seams in one direction.

Figure 3

5. Sew a C rectangle to each side of the Flying Geese strip as shown in Figure 4; press seams toward C.

Figure 4

6. Sew D to the Flying Geese unit to complete the outer wallet; press seam toward D.

7. Bond a 9½" x 17½" rectangle fusible fleece to the wrong side of the outer wallet. Quilt as desired.

8. Center and glue-baste the loop side of the 4" length of hook-and-loop tape 6" up from bottom edge of outer wallet as shown in Figure 5. Stitch all edges to hold.

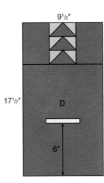

Figure 5

Completing the Inner Wallet

1. Fold and press the Q binding strip in half lengthwise. Fold and press long edges to center then repress center fold to make double-fold binding strip. Apply binding along one 2¾" edge of the vinyl piece and topstitch in place. **Do not press!**

2. Sandwich the 2¾" unbound end of the vinyl piece between the L and K pieces and stitch. Open seam and finger-press flat to make the license pocket band as shown in Figure 6.

vinyl

Figure 6

3. Sew M strips to opposite long sides of the license pocket band to complete the inner top band referring to Figure 7. Carefully press from the wrong side with seams toward M. **Note:** *Be careful not to melt vinyl when pressing!*

Figure 7

4. Bond a ½" x 3½" strip fusible fleece centered on the wrong side of a P strip. Fold one long edge of P over the fleece strip.

5. Fold the remaining long edge of P ¼" to wrong side and fold over to cover raw edge. Edgestitch center fold of strip in place.

6. Thread strip through a D-ring. Match and stitch raw ends together to make a P loop.

7. Repeat steps 4–6 to make a second P loop.

8. Pin and baste a P loop ½" in from each end of the J 9½" edge as shown in Figure 8. **Note:** *Use painters tape to hold P loops in place when sewing.*

Figure 8

9. Sew J loop edge to the license pocket band to complete the inside of the wallet.

10. Bond the second 9½" x 13½" rectangle fusible fleece to wrong side of inside wallet.

11. Center and glue-baste the hook side of the 4" length of hook-and-loop tape ½" down from top of M on license pocket section as shown in Figure 9; stitch all around to hold.

Figure 9

12. Center and glue-baste the hook side of the 8¼" length of hook-and-loop tape ¾" down from M/J seam, again referring to Figure 9; stitch all around to hold.

Completing the Wallet Flap

1. Bond the 9½" squares of fusible interfacing to the wrong sides of N and O.

2. Fold and press the E, F and G rectangles in half lengthwise wrong sides together.

3. Layer F on G and E on F, matching raw edges. Pin and baste to the bottom and side edges of O as shown in Figure 10.

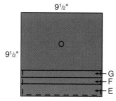

Figure 10

4. Fold the H rectangle in half lengthwise right sides together. Fuse a 3" x 9½" fusible fleece rectangle to one side. Stitch long raw edges together leaving ends open. Turn right side out to make the H pocket; press flat and topstitch ¼" from top edge.

5. Position H pocket 2" down from top edge of O, matching edges as shown in Figure 11. Baste side edges then topstitch across long bottom edge of H to secure, again referring to Figure 11.

Figure 11

6. Place the O pocket flap right sides together with N pocket backing and stitch across top edge. Separately stitch the side and bottom edges below the H pocket as shown in Figure 12. Clip seam allowance just below H pocket seam.

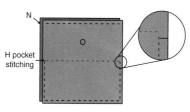

Figure 12

7. Turn right side out and press flat. **Note:** *The G/F/E pocket section is now finished around the side and bottom edges but the H pocket section is left unfinished* *as shown in Figure 13. The H pocket section edges will be included in the wallet binding, allowing the G/F/E pocket section to flip up.*

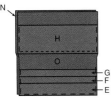

Figure 13

8. To make credit-card pockets, stitch 3¾" in from each side of G/F/E pocket section as shown in Figure 14. ***Note:*** *Tiny center pockets could hold subway tokens, address labels, stamps, dental floss, etc.*

Figure 14

9. Glue-baste and stitch the hook side of the 8½" length of hook-and-loop tape ¼" from the top on the N side of the O pocket flap.

Completing the Wallet

Project Note: *You may need to switch to a Denim/Jeans 14-18 needle to successfully stitch the multiple layers in this section.*

1. With fleece sides together and edges even, machine-baste the outer wallet and inner wallet layers together to hold.

2. Fold and press the R binding strip wrong sides together lengthwise.

3. Pin the raw edge of the folded binding strip to the un-pieced end of the basted wallet layers and stitch.

4. Fold the binding to the wrong side and hand- or machine-stitch in place to finish edge.

5. Fold the bound edge 3½" to the J inner wallet side to form a pocket as shown in Figure 15; machine-baste in place at side edges.

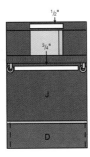

Figure 15

6. Pin the finished O pocket flap to inner wallet ½" below the M/J seam as shown in Figure 16, matching up hook-and-loop tape for the secure closed pocket.

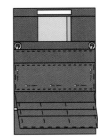

Figure 16

7. Stitch O pocket flap to J ¼" from bottom of pocket H referring to Figure 17.

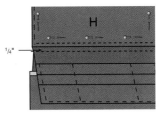

Figure 17

8. Join the bias binding strips on short ends with diagonal seams to make a long strip; trim seams to ¼" and press open.

9. Fold and press binding strip in half lengthwise wrong sides together. Fold and press one short end ¼" to wrong side.

10. Starting with folded short end, matching raw edges to outside wallet edges, stitch binding to wallet around the three sides, trimming binding end ¼" longer than wallet sides length and turning end under before reaching the end.

11. Turn binding to the inner wallet side and hand- or machine-stitch in place.

12. Join the S strips on short ends to make one strip. Trim to 54".

13. Center and bond the ½"-wide strips fusible fleece to center of S strip. Fold S strip ends in ¼" and press.

14. Fold and press one long edge over the fleece. Fold the remaining long edge ¼" to the wrong side and press. Press this edge over to cover the previously folded side and edgestitch all edges of strap to finish.

15. Insert the ends of the strap into the end of the swivel snap hooks 1" and stitch strap to itself to secure.

16. Insert the swivel snap hook into the D-rings to complete the wallet. ■

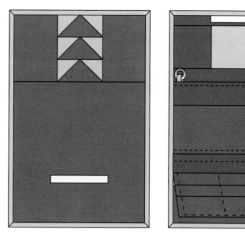

Wild Goose Chase Wallet
Placement Diagram
9 x 4½" folded; 9 x 13½" open flat

Cracker Box

This album quilt is easily expandable by adding more blocks. It's the perfect gift for graduations and weddings. All the guests can sign a block.

DESIGN BY RUTH SWASEY

PROJECT SPECIFICATIONS

Skill Level: Beginner
Wall Quilt Size: 29" x 29"
Block Size: 4" x 4"
Number of Blocks: 36

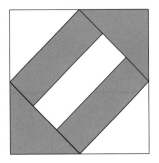

Cracker Box
4" x 4" Block
Make 36

MATERIALS

- Scraps of 36 different prints
- ⅝ yard solid white
- ⅔ yard coordinating print
- Backing 33" x 33"
- Batting 33" x 33"
- Coordinating color all purpose thread
- Natural-color quilting thread
- Template material or poster board
- Fine-tip permanent fabric marking pen (coordinating color)
- Basic sewing tools and supplies

Cutting

1. Prepare templates from template material or poster board using pattern pieces A and B on page 67.

2. Choose same-color scraps and cut two each A and B. Repeat to cut 36 pairs of A and B pieces.

3. Cut 72 A triangles and 36 B rectangles from solid white using templates.

4. Cut four 3" by fabric width strips coordinating print; subcut into two 3" x 24½" C borders and two 3" x 29½" D borders.

5. Cut three 2¼" by fabric width coordinating print strips for binding.

Completing the Block

1. Choose an A/B print pair, one B solid white and two A solid white pieces to make one Cracker Box block.

2. Sew a white B between two same-print B pieces to make a B unit as shown in Figure 1; press seams toward B prints.

Figure 1

3. Sew two same-print A triangles to opposite sides of the B unit (Figure 2). Press seams toward the triangles.

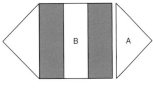

Figure 2

4. Sew two solid white A triangles to remaining opposite sides of the B unit (Figure 3). Press seams toward the B unit to complete a Cracker Box block.

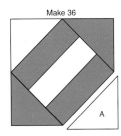

Make 36

Figure 3

5. Repeat steps 1–4 to make 36 blocks each using a different same-print pair of A/B pieces.

Completing the Top

1. Choose six Cracker Box blocks and sew together, matching the white triangles to form a chevron patterned row referring to Figure 4. Press seams in one direction. Repeat to make six rows, pressing seams in alternate directions.

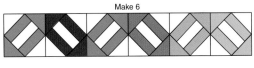

Make 6

Figure 4

2. Sew rows together, matching colored triangles to solid white triangles referring to Figure 5 and matching seams. Press seams in one direction.

Figure 5

3. Referring to the Placement Diagram, sew 3" x 24½" C borders to the top and bottom of the pieced center; press seams toward border.

4. Sew 3" x 29½" D borders to the sides of the pieced center; press seams toward border.

5. Press quilt top on both sides; check for proper seam pressing and trim all loose threads.

6. Sandwich batting between the stitched top and the prepared backing piece; pin or baste layers together to hold.

7. Quilt-in-the-ditch around the solid B piece of the block (Figure 6). Choose a fine-tip permanent fabric marking pen in a darker coordinating color. Have family and guests at a birthday, graduation, wedding or anniversary party sign in the solid B piece, again referring to Figure 6. Follow manufacturer's instructions to permanently set the fabric marker's ink.

Figure 6

8. When quilting is complete, remove pins or basting. Trim batting and backing fabric edges even with raw edges of quilt top.

9. Join binding strips on short ends with diagonal seams to make one long strip; trim seams to ¼" and press seams open.

10. Fold the binding strip in half with wrong sides together along length; press.

11. Sew binding to quilt edges, matching raw edges, mitering corners and overlapping ends.

12. Fold binding to the back side and stitch in place to finish. ■

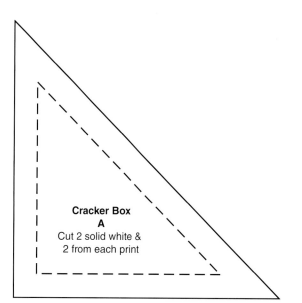

Cracker Box
A
Cut 2 solid white &
2 from each print

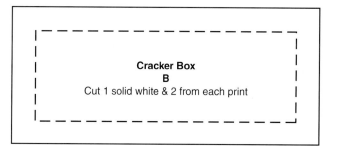

Cracker Box
B
Cut 1 solid white & 2 from each print

Cracker Box
Placement Diagram 29" x 29"

May Day Tulip Place Mat

Practice both paper piecing and machine quilting with these easy place mat and napkin projects!

DESIGN BY KATE LAUCOMER

PROJECT SPECIFICATIONS

Skill Level: Beginner
Place Mat Size: 18" x 12"
Napkin Size: 18" x 18"

PROJECT NOTE

Materials listed and instructions are for two place mats and two napkins.

MATERIALS

- 1⅔ yards green print
- ⅛ yard cream print
- Scraps yellow print
- Batting: 2 (19" x 13") rectangles
- 2 (8½" x 11") foundation or tissue paper
- Scraps paper-backed fusible web
- All-purpose thread
- Natural-colored quilting thread
- Variegated thread (optional)
- Basic sewing tools and supplies

Cutting

1. Cut one 12½" by fabric width strip from green print. Subcut strip into two 12½" x 14½" A rectangles.

2. Cut one 19" by fabric width strip from green print. Subcut into two 19" B squares.

3. Cut one 13" by fabric width strip from green print. Subcut strip into two 13" x 19" rectangles for place mat backing.

4. Cut four 2½" by fabric width strips from green print for binding.

5. Cut two 2½" x 4½" C rectangles from cream print scrap.

Paper-Piecing Tulip and Leaf & Stem Units

1. Trace or copy two each tulip and leaf & stem paper-piecing patterns on pages 72 and 73 onto foundation or tissue paper.

2. Layer a yellow and cream scrap that are at least ¼" larger all around than areas labeled piece 1 and 2 on the tulip paper foundation pattern, right sides together. Position and pin the scraps under piece 1 of the paper pattern (Figure 1).

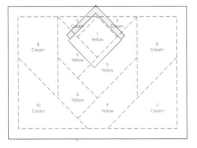

Figure 1

3. Set your sewing machine stitch length on 18 to 20 stitches per inch. ***Note:*** *Stitching at a short stitch length helps perforate the paper, making it easier to remove when piecing is completed.*

4. Sew along the line between piece 1 and 2, extending the stitching ¼" beyond the end of the line (Figure 2). Trim seam allowance to approximately ¼" from stitching referring to Figure 3. Press piece 2 fabric away from piece 1 (Figure 4).

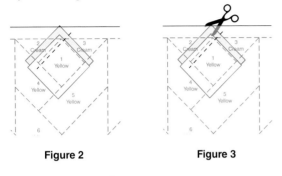

| Figure 2 | Figure 3 |

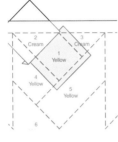

Figure 4

5. Repeat steps 2–4 referring to the tulip and leaf & stem patterns for color and numerical order to add scraps to complete the paper-pieced units.

Completing the Place Mat

1. Remove paper and sew a tulip section to top of a leaf-and-stem section as shown in Figure 5. Press seam toward tulip section. Repeat to make two complete tulip units.

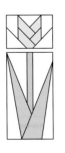

| Figure 5 | Figure 6 |

2. Sew a C rectangle to the top of each tulip unit (Figure 6). Press seam toward C.

3. Sew a tulip unit to right short side of A rectangle (Figure 7). Press seam allowance toward green fabric. Repeat to make two place mats.

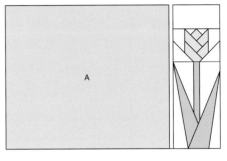

Figure 7

4. Trace three tulip quilting patterns, found on page 73, evenly onto the A rectangle of each place mat top referring to the Placement Diagram.

5. Press place mat tops on both sides; check for proper seam pressing and trim all loose threads.

6. Sandwich batting between the stitched top and the prepared backing piece; pin or baste layers together to hold. Quilt on marked lines and as desired by hand or machine.

7. When quilting is complete, remove pins or basting. Trim batting and backing fabric edges even with raw edges of quilt top.

8. Join binding strips on short ends with diagonal seams to make one long strip; trim seams to ¼" and press seams open.

9. Fold the binding strip in half with wrong sides together along length; press.

10. Sew binding to quilt edges, matching raw edges, mitering corners and overlapping ends.

11. Fold binding to the back side and stitch in place to finish.

Completing the Napkins

1. Turn all B square edges under ¼" and press. Turn edges under another ¼"; press and topstitch to make a double-turned ¼" hem all around.

2. Fold each napkin in half diagonally once and press.

3. To make tulip appliqué, trace two tulip shapes, from the tulip paper-piecing pattern, onto the paper side of paper-backed fusible web about ½" apart (Figure 8).

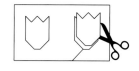

Figure 8

4. Cut out, leaving approximately ¼" margin around each shape, again referring to Figure 8. Follow manufacturer's instructions and fuse to yellow print scraps. Cut out on traced lines.

5. Referring to Figure 9 and the Placement Diagram, position tulip appliqués on lower right corner of each napkin approximately 1¼" from corner point, centering on diagonally pressed line. Fuse in place.

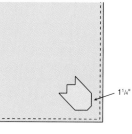

Figure 9

6. Stitch around the tulip appliqué in a variegated or natural-colored thread using a narrow machine buttonhole or satin stitch. ▨

May Day Tulip Napkin
Placement Diagram 18" x 18"

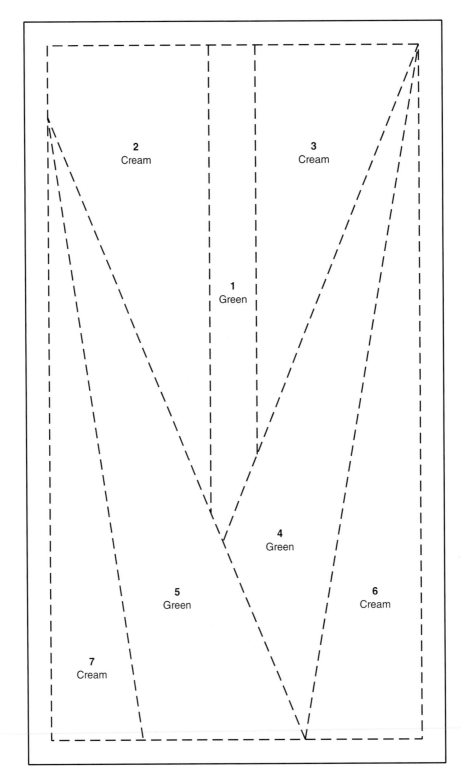

Leaf & Stem Paper-Piecing Pattern

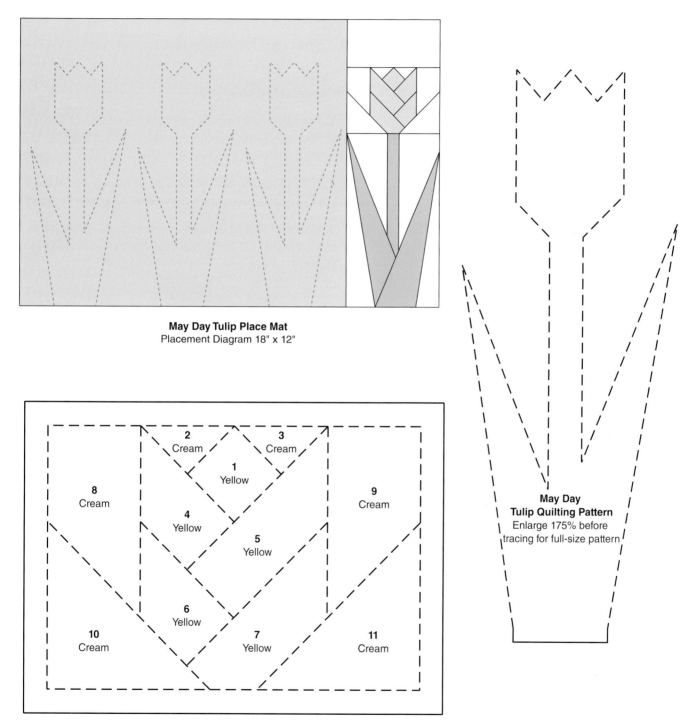

May Day Tulip Place Mat
Placement Diagram 18" x 12"

Tulip Paper-Piecing Pattern

**May Day
Tulip Quilting Pattern**
Enlarge 175% before
tracing for full-size pattern

Daisy Pocket Quilt

Sorting summertime items is easier with this simple pocket quilt.

DESIGN BY PHYLLIS DOBBS

PROJECT SPECIFICATIONS

Skill Level: Beginner
Quilt Size: 42" x 52"

MATERIALS

- ⅔ yard multicolored squares print
- ⅔ yard purple print
- 1 yard green print
- 1⅛ yards pink print
- 1⅜ yards yellow print
- Backing 48" x 58"
- Batting 48" x 58"
- Neutral-color all-purpose thread
- Multicolored quilting thread
- 1 yard fusible web
- Basic sewing tools and supplies

Cutting

1. Cut two 9½" by fabric width strips from multi-colored squares print; subcut eight 9½" C squares.

2. Cut two 4½" x 26½" E strips from purple print.

3. Cut two 11½" x 26½" B rectangles from green print.

4. Cut one 4½" by fabric width strip from green print; subcut into four 4½" x 8½" F rectangles.

5. Cut two 11½" x 26½" A rectangles from pink print.

6. Cut five 2¼" by fabric width strips from pink print for binding.

7. Cut two 8½" x 44½" D strips along fabric length from yellow print.

Completing the Quilt

1. Trace the daisy motifs onto the paper side of the fusible web as directed on pattern; cut out shapes, leaving a margin around each one.

2. Fuse shapes to the wrong side of fabrics as directed; cut out shapes on traced lines. Remove paper backing.

3. Fold each A and B rectangle in half and crease to mark the vertical and horizontal centers as shown in Figure 1.

Figure 1

4. Center and fuse a flower motif to the left side of the crease on A referring to Figure 2. Repeat on the second A.

Figure 2

5. Repeat step 4 with a flower motif on the right side of each B rectangle.

6. Machine buttonhole-stitch around fused shapes to hold in place.

7. Place two C squares right sides together; stitch all around, leaving a 3" opening on one side. Clip corners and turn right side out. Repeat with all C squares.

8. Turn in the openings on each C unit ¼"; press and hand-stitch openings closed to complete four C pockets.

9. Center and pin the C pockets on the right side of each A rectangle and on the left side of each B rectangle referring to Figure 3 for positioning.

Figure 3

10. Stitch C pockets in place, sewing around three sides and leaving the top edge open.

11. Join the A and B rectangles referring to the Placement Diagram for positioning; press seams in one direction.

12. Sew an E strip to the top and bottom of the pieced section; press seams toward E strips.

13. Sew an F strip to each short end of D; press seams toward D. Repeat to make two D-F strips.

14. Sew a D-F strip to opposite long sides of the pieced center; press seams toward D-F strips.

15. Press quilt top on both sides; check for proper seam pressing and trim all loose threads.

16. Sandwich batting between the stitched top and the prepared backing piece; pin or baste layers together to hold. Quilt on marked lines and as desired by hand or machine.

17. When quilting is complete, remove pins or basting. Trim batting and backing fabric edges even with raw edges of quilt top.

18. Join binding strips on short ends with diagonal seams to make one long strip; trim seams to ¼" and press seams open.

19. Fold the binding strip in half with wrong sides together along length; press.

20. Sew binding to quilt edges, matching raw edges, mitering corners and overlapping ends.

21. Fold binding to the back side and stitch in place to finish.

22. Add a fabric sleeve or bone rings to the back top edge for hanging, if desired. ■

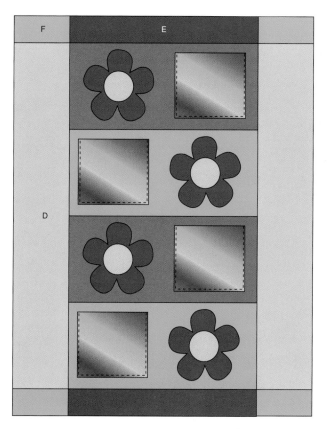

Daisy Pocket Quilt
Placement Diagram 42" x 52"

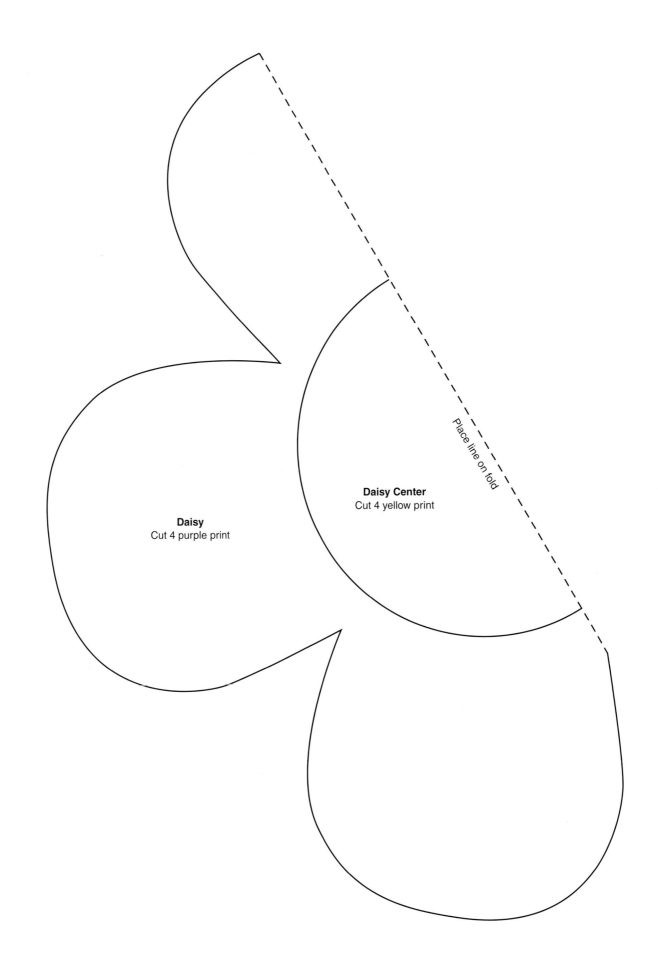

Daisy
Cut 4 purple print

Daisy Center
Cut 4 yellow print

Place line on fold

Cellphone Carrier

This little paper-pieced cellphone carrier makes a wonderful gift for anyone who can't part with their mobile device.

DESIGN BY KATE LAUCOMER

PROJECT SPECIFICATIONS

Skill Level: Intermediate
Carrier Size: Size Varies

MATERIALS

- Variety bright-colored scraps
- 1 fat eighth coordinating solid
- 1 fat quarter lime green tonal
- Batting 8" x 6" (size varies)
- All-purpose thread
- Scrap fabric stabilizer
- Paper
- Basic sewing tools and supplies

Cutting

1. Measure around the width of your cellphone; add ¾" to the width measurement.

2. Measure the length of your cellphone; add ½" to the length measurement. **Note:** *The average size of a cellphone is 2" wide, 4" tall and ¾" deep.* If you want your cellphone to fit down inside the carrier and not extend out at the top, add 1" to the length instead of ½".

3. Cut one rectangle each from coordinating solid for lining and lime green tonal (A) the sizes determined in steps 1 and 2.

4. Cut one 1" x 6½" (or 9") from lime green tonal for strap.

5. Cut one 2" x 12" strip from lime green tonal for binding.

Completing the Flying Geese Paper-Pieced Unit

1. Make two copies of the Flying Geese paper-piecing pattern on page 81. Cut up one copy to make templates for the pieces; using the paper patterns, cut pieces for each shape, adding ½" all around when cutting. **Note:** *You don't have to be exact when cutting these pieces; they are just guides to make sure your pieces are large enough to cover the spaces on the paper-piecing pattern.*

2. Set machine stitch length to 15 stitches per inch or 1.5.

3. Pin piece 1 right side up in the number 1 position on the unmarked side of the paper.

4. Place piece 2 right sides together with piece 1; stitch on the 1–2 line on the marked side of the paper as shown in Figure 1. Press piece 2 to the right side.

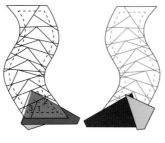

Figure 1

5. Repeat step 4 with all pieces in numerical order to complete the Flying Geese unit; press all pieces to the right side after stitching.

6. Trim the pieced unit on the outside line.

7. Pin the scrap of fabric stabilizer to the right side of the Flying Geese unit; stitch along both long sides using a ¼" seam allowance.

8. Remove paper backing from the Flying Geese unit.

9. Trim stabilizer slightly wider than the edge of the Flying Geese unit; turn right side out through one end opening. Press edges flat. ***Note:*** *If stabilizer pulls on the Flying Geese unit, cut a slit down the center of the stabilizer the length of the Flying Geese unit.*

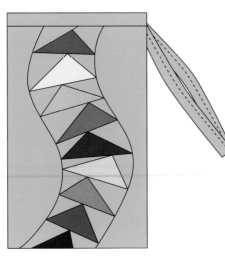

Cellphone Carrier
Placement Diagram Size Varies

Completing the Cellphone Carrier

1. Cut the batting piece ½" narrower and ½" shorter than the A piece.

2. Layer lining right side down, batting and A right side up; hand- or machine-quilt layers together.

3. Fold the quilted piece A along the long sides and crease to mark the center.

4. Center and pin the Flying Geese unit along the creased centerline of the A piece as shown in Figure 2. ***Note:*** *If the Flying Geese unit is not long enough, add a piece of the background fabric to the top or bottom of the unit.*

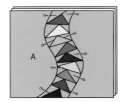

Figure 2

5. Hand- or machine-stitch the Flying Geese unit to the A side of the quilted piece.

6. Serge or machine zigzag the short ends of the quilted piece.

7. Fold in half with short ends right sides together; sew ¼" seam from top to bottom; press seam open.

8. Find the center mark creased in step 3; align with the stitched seam and pin to hold as shown in Figure 3. Stitch along pinned edges with a ¼" seam to close the bottom; serge seam or cover with a tight machine zigzag. Turn right side out.

Figure 3

9. Fold the long edges of the strap piece ¼" to the inside; press. Fold in half again; press and stitch close to edge to finish the strap.

10. Fold the strap in half and pin at the top edge on one side as shown in Figure 4; machine-baste to hold in place.

Figure 4

11. Measure around the top edge of the carrier; add ½" to this measurement.

12. Trim the 2" x 12" binding strip to this length; sew together on the short ends. Press seam open.

13. Fold stitched binding in half to make a double layer; press.

14. Pin the folded binding to the top edge of the carrier matching raw edges. Stitch all around; press binding up and turn to the lining side. Hand-stitch in place to finish. ■

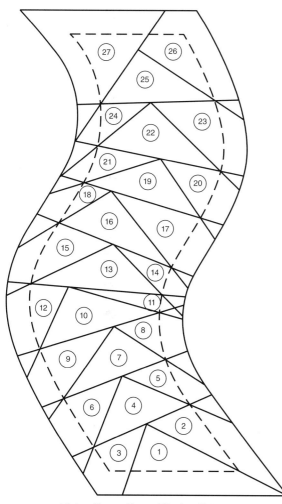

Flying Geese Paper-Piecing Pattern
Make 2 copies
Cut pieces 1, 4, 7, 10, 13, 16, 19, 22 & 25 from bright scraps
Cut all other pieces from lime green tonal

17-Hour Sensations

Quilters love to use their scraps to create both decorative and functional projects. In this chapter you will find quilts, holiday pot holders, covers for your electronic devices and much more. Use your special stash or scraps to create quilted masterpieces that you can give as gifts or keep for yourself. Fun and easy, these 17-hour projects will be done before you know it!

Color Wheel Runner

Divide your fabric scraps into lights and darks to make this bed runner.
The more colors you use, the more movement your finished quilt will show.

DESIGN BY CONNIE RAND

PROJECT SPECIFICATIONS

Skill Level: Intermediate
Quilt Size: 74" x 23"
Block Size: 17" x 17"
Number of Blocks: 4

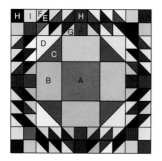

Color Wheel
17" x 17" Block
Make 4

MATERIALS

- Variety light and dark 2½" strips to total at least nine 2½" x 42" strips each
- Assorted light and dark scraps for H and I (at least 2½" square)
- 8 (5") squares green tonal
- 8 (5") squares light tonal
- 1 fat quarter red tonal
- ½ yard pink tonal
- ⅝ yard dark blue tonal
- Batting 86" x 32"
- Backing 86" x 32"
- Neutral-color all-purpose thread
- Quilting thread
- Template material
- Basic sewing tools and supplies

Cutting

1. Cut (96) 2½" squares from dark precut strips. Cut each square in half on one diagonal to make 192 E triangles.

2. Cut (80) 2½" squares from light precut strips. Cut each square in half on one diagonal to make 160 F triangles.

3. Cut one 2½" by fabric width strip pink tonal; subcut strip into (16) 2½" squares. Cut each square in half on one diagonal to make 32 G triangles.

4. Cut five 3½" by fabric width K/L strips dark blue tonal.

5. Prepare templates for remaining pieces using patterns on page 86. Cut pieces as instructed on each piece.

Completing the Blocks

1. Sew H to I to make an H-I unit as shown in Figure 1; press seam toward H. Repeat to make 32 H-I units.

Corner Unit
Make 16

Make 32

Figure 1

2. Join two H-I units to make a corner unit, again referring to Figure 1; press seams in one direction. Repeat to make 16 H-I corner units.

3. Sew E to F along the diagonal; press seam toward E. Repeat to make 160 E-F units (Figure 2).

Make 160

Figure 2

4. Sew E to G along the diagonal to make an E-G unit as shown in Figure 3; press seam toward E. Repeat to make 32 E-G units, again referring to Figure 3.

Make 32

Figure 3

5. Referring to Figure 4, join three E-F units to make a row; press seams toward the F side of the row. Join two E-F units and one E-G unit to make a second row, again referring to Figure 4.

Half-Square Unit
Make 32

Figure 4

6. Join the rows made in step 5 to make a half-square unit as shown in Figure 4; press seam in one direction

7. Repeat steps 5 and 6 to make 32 half-square units.

8. Sew an H to a J square to make a center unit (Figure 5); press seam toward H Repeat to make 16 center units.

Center Unit
Make 16

Figure 5

9. Sew a center unit between two half-square units with G next to J as shown in Figure 6 to make a block side unit; press seams toward the center unit Repeat to make 16 block side units.

Block Side Unit
Make 16

Figure 6

10. To make a block top/bottom unit, join two corner units and a block side unit as shown in Figure 7; press seams away from the corner units Repeat to make eight block top/bottom units.

Block Top/Bottom Unit
Make 8

Figure 7

11. Sew C to D along the diagonal to make a C-D unit; press seam toward C. Repeat to make two C-D units.

12. Sew a C-D unit to each end of B to make a B-C-D unit; press seams toward B (Figure 8). Repeat to make eight B-C-D units.

B-C-D Unit
Make 8

Figure 8

13. Sew B to opposite sides of A to make an A-B unit (Figure 9); press seams toward B. Repeat to make four A-B units.

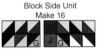

A-B Unit
Make 4

Figure 9

14. Sew a B-C-D unit to the top and bottom of an A-B unit, as shown in Figure 10, to make a block center; press seams toward the A-B unit. Repeat to make four block centers.

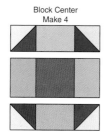

Block Center
Make 4

Figure 10

15. Referring to Figure 11, sew a block side unit to opposite sides of a block center; press seams toward block center.

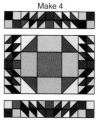

Make 4

Figure 11

16. Sew block top/bottom units to the block center as shown in Figure 11 to complete one Color Wheel block; press seams toward the block center

17. Repeat steps 15 and 16 to make four blocks.

Completing the Quilt Top

1. Join the four Color Wheel blocks in a row to complete the pieced center referring to the Placement Diagram for positioning; press seams in one direction.

2. Join the K/L strips on short ends; press seams in one direction. Subcut strip into two 18½" K strips and two 74½" L strips.

3. Sew K strips to short ends of the pieced center; press seams toward K. Sew L strips to top and bottom of the pieced center to complete the pieced top; press seams toward L.

Completing the Quilt

1. Press quilt top on both sides; check for proper seam, pressing and trim all loose threads.

2. Sandwich batting between the stitched top and the prepared backing piece; pin or baste layers together to hold. Quilt on marked lines and as desired by hand or machine.

3. When quilting is complete, remove pins or basting. Trim batting and backing fabric edges even with raw edges of quilt top.

4. Join binding strips on short ends with diagonal seams to make one long strip; trim seams to ¼" and press seams open. ***Note:*** *Leftover dark tonal 2½" strips were used for binding on the sample.*

5. Fold the binding strip in half with wrong sides together along length; press.

6. Sew binding to quilt edges, matching raw edges, mitering corners and overlapping ends.

7. Fold binding to the back side and stitch in place to finish. ■

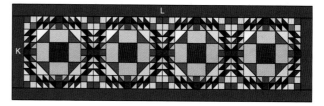

Color Wheel Bed Runner
Placement Diagram 74" x 23"

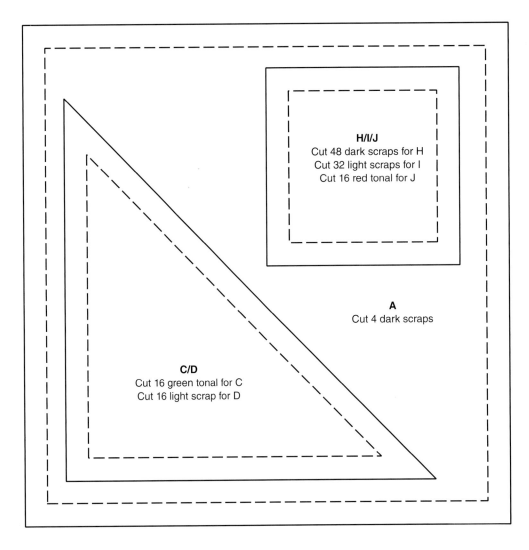

H/I/J
Cut 48 dark scraps for H
Cut 32 light scraps for I
Cut 16 red tonal for J

A
Cut 4 dark scraps

C/D
Cut 16 green tonal for C
Cut 16 light scrap for D

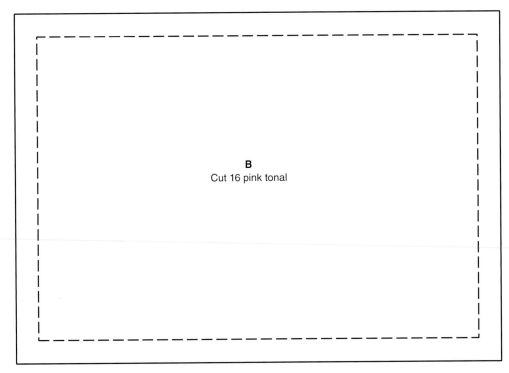

B
Cut 16 pink tonal

Jolly Santa Pot Holder

This delightful Santa is perfect for gift-giving or to lend Christmas cheer to your own kitchen.

DESIGN BY BARBARA CLAYTON

PROJECT SPECIFICATIONS

Skill Level: Beginner
Pot Holder Size: Approximately 8" x 8¾"

MATERIALS

- Scraps red, medium rose, light rose, peach and green
- ⅜ yard white tonal
- 9" x 9¾" rectangle heat-resistant batting
- All-purpose thread to match fabrics
- Clear nylon monofilament
- Black and white quilting thread
- White paper
- Small wisps polyester fiberfill
- Scraps fusible interfacing
- Basic sewing tools and supplies

Cutting and Preparing Appliqué Pieces

1. Cut Santa face, mouth, nose, hat and holly berries as directed on pattern (pages 174 & 175).

2. Trace Santa cheeks, mustache, hat trim, beard and holly leaves onto the smooth side of the fusible interfacing as directed on patterns, leaving ½" between pieces when tracing.

3. Cut out shapes, leaving a margin around each one.

4. Pin the fusible side of the marked interfacing on the right side of the fabrics as directed on patterns for color.

5. Stitch on the marked lines of the hat trim, mustache and holly leaves only. Cut out ⅛" beyond the stitched lines as shown in Figure 1; trim points and clip curves.

⅛"

Figure 1

6. Make a small slash through the center of the interfacing only and turn each piece right side out. Using a sharp object, carefully smooth out the seams on the inside of each piece.

7. Stitch only between the dots as marked on cheeks and beard pieces; trim seams and turn right side out.

8. Transfer quilting lines onto the mustache, beard and holly leaves referring to the pattern.

9. Transfer eyes to the Santa face using a pencil. Pin a small piece of white paper to the wrong side of the Santa face to stabilize.

10. Using black thread, stitch the traced eyes using a medium-width zigzag stitch.

11. Position and pin the Santa mouth and Santa hat on the face, overlapping edges as shown in pattern.

Completing the Appliqué

1. Position and pin the Santa mouth and Santa hat on the face, overlapping edges as shown in pattern.

2. Referring to the Placement Diagram, place the cheeks on the face and fuse in place using a medium-hot iron.

3. Using clear nylon monofilament in the needle and white thread in the bobbin, stitch around each appliqué shape using a narrow blind hemstitch.

4. Pin the beard to the face, then place the mustache pieces, hat trim and holly leaves on the beard referring to the pattern for positioning.

5. Fuse and blind hemstitch in place as in step 3.

Completing the Pot Holder

1. Hand-stitch around the nose shape ¼" from edges; pull up the threads to gather as shown in Figure 2.

Figure 2

2. Stuff the gathered nose shape lightly with polyester fiberfill.

3. Gather the nose circle closed and stitch to secure.

4. Repeat steps 1–3 with the three holly berry shapes.

5. Cut one 2" x 4¾" strip for hanging tab. Fold strip in half along length with wrong sides together and press to form a crease.

6. Fold the raw edges to the center crease line and press again; topstitch close to the open edge to finish the loop strip as shown in Figure 3.

Figure 3

7. Fold the loop strip with ends together to form a loop, matching raw ends and baste as shown in Figure 4.

Figure 4

8. Center and baste the loop on the top of the hat as shown in Figure 5.

Figure 5

9. Cut a 9" x 9¾" rectangle from the remaining white tonal. Place the completed Santa face right sides together on the white tonal rectangle and pin to hold; place the pinned layers to the batting rectangle and stitch around the completed Santa face ¼" from edges all around, leaving a small opening on the edges of the beard as indicated on pattern.

10. Trim excess batting and backing even with the edges of the Santa face; clip points and curves.

11. Turn right side out through opening, pulling tab loop up; hand-stitch opening closed.

12. Using white quilting thread, hand-quilt ¼" from edge of red hat, on traced lines on the holly leaves and in the ditch of seams between hat and hat trim.

13. Using black quilting thread, hand-quilt ¼" from the edges of the hat trim and beard, in the ditch between face parts and on traced quilting lines on the beard and mustache pieces to finish. ■

Patterns continued on page 174

Pathways Prayer Shawl

This fresh, quilted prayer shawl would make a wonderful gift for an ailing friend and later could be used as a cheerful bed runner.

DESIGN BY GINA GEMPESAW
QUILTED BY CAROLE WHALING

PROJECT SPECIFICATIONS

Skill Level: Beginner
Shawl Size: 72" x 36"
Block Size: 18" x 18"
Number of Blocks: 8

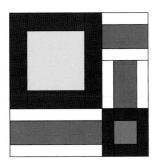

Pathways
18" x 18" Block
Make 8

MATERIALS

- ½ yard large print
- ⅔ yard small print
- ⅔ yard coordinating medium
- ¾ yard coordinating light
- 1¼ yards coordinating dark
- Backing 80" x 44"
- Batting 80" x 44"
- Neutral-color all-purpose thread
- Quilting thread
- Basic sewing tools and supplies

Cutting

1. Cut two 8" by fabric width A strips large print.

2. Cut one 3½" by fabric width F strip small print.

3. Cut six 2¼" by fabric width strips small print for binding.

4. Cut six 3½" by fabric width G strips coordinating medium.

5. Cut (12) 2" by fabric width H strips coordinating light.

6. Cut (10) 2¾" by fabric width B strips coordinating dark. Subcut six B strips into (16) 2¾" x 12½" C strips.

7. Cut five 2" by fabric width D strips coordinating dark. Subcut three D strips into (16) 2" x 6½" E strips.

Completing the Blocks

1. Sew an A strip between two B strips to make a B-A-B strip set (Figure 1); press seams toward A. Repeat to make a second strip set.

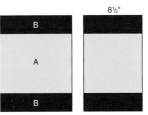

Figure 1

2. From strip sets cut eight 8½" B-A-B rectangles, again referring to Figure 1.

3. Sew a C strip to opposite sides of a B-A-B rectangle as shown in Figure 2 to make an A-B-C unit; press seams toward C. Repeat to make eight A-B-C units.

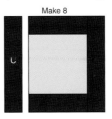

Figure 2

4. Sew an F strip between two D strips to make a D-F-D strip set; press seams toward F. Subcut the strip set into eight 3½" D-F-D pieces (Figure 3).

Figure 3

5. Sew an E strip to opposite sides of a D-F-D rectangle to make a D-F-E unit (Figure 4); press seams toward E. Repeat to make eight D-F-E units.

Make 8

Figure 4

6. Sew a G strip between two H strips to make an H-G-H strip set; press seams toward G. Repeat to make six strip sets. Subcut three strip sets into eight 12½" H-G-H units (Figure 5). Subcut the remaining three strip sets into (16) 6½" H-G-H units (Figure 6).

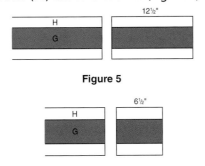

Figure 5

Figure 6

7. Join two 6½" H-G-H units to make an H-G-H section as shown in Figure 7; press seams toward top unit. Repeat to make eight H-G-H sections.

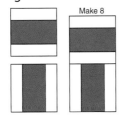

Make 8

Figure 7

8. To complete one Pathways block, select and join one A-B-C unit and one H-G-H section to make a top section as shown in Figure 8; press seam toward A-B-C unit.

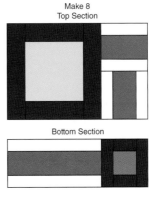

Make 8
Top Section

Bottom Section

Figure 8

9. Select and join one D-E-F unit and one 12½" H-G-H unit to make the bottom section, again referring to Figure 8; press seam toward D-E-F unit. Join the pieced sections referring to the block drawing to make one Pathways block; press seams to one side.

10. Repeat steps 7–9 to make eight Pathways blocks.

Completing the Bed Runner

1. Join four Pathways blocks to make a row, rotating the blocks as shown in Figure 9; press seams in one direction. Repeat to make a second row, again referring to Figure 9.

Figure 9

2. Join the rows referring to Placement Diagram to complete the show top.

3. Press quilt top on both sides; check for proper seam pressing and trim all loose threads.

4. Sandwich batting between the stitched top and the prepared backing piece; pin or baste layers together to hold. Quilt on marked lines and as desired by hand or machine.

5. When quilting is complete, remove pins or basting. Trim batting and backing fabric edges even with raw edges of shawl top.

6. Join binding strips on short ends with diagonal seams to make one long strip; trim seams to ¼" and press seams open.

7. Fold the binding strip in half with wrong sides together along length; press.

8. Sew binding to quilt edges, matching raw edges, mitering corners and overlapping ends.

9. Fold binding to the back side and stitch in place to finish. ■

Pathways Prayer Shawl
Placement Diagram 72" x 36"

Dots Done Your Way

Polka-dotted fabrics and circles create the design in this easy baby quilt.

DESIGN BY JOAN BALLARD

PROJECT SPECIFICATIONS

Skill Level: Beginner
Quilt Size: 43½" x 50"
Block Size: 6½" x 6½" and 5½" x 5½"
Number of Blocks: 30 and 4

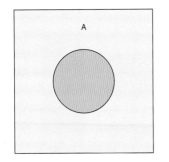

Circle
6½" x 6½"
Make 30

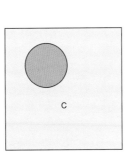

Corner
5½" x 5½"
Make 4

MATERIALS

- ⅝ yard each peach, blue, pink and green polka dots
- 1 yard yellow polka dot
- Backing 50" x 56"
- Batting 50" x 56"
- Cream all-purpose thread
- ⅞ yard 18"-wide fusible web
- 1 yard fabric stabilizer
- Basic sewing tools and supplies

Cutting

1. Cut one 7" by fabric width strip each from peach, blue and green polka dots. Subcut each strip into six 7" A squares.

2. Cut one 6" by fabric width strip each from peach, blue and green polka dots. Subcut a variety of 2"–3½" wide B strips from each strip.

3. Cut one 7" by fabric width strip from pink polka dots; subcut into six 7" A squares.

4. Cut one 6" by fabric width strip from pink polka dots; subcut into two 6" C squares and a variety of 2"–3½"-wide B strips.

5. Cut one 7" by fabric width strip from yellow polka dots; subcut into six 7" A squares.

6. Cut one 6" by fabric width strip from yellow polka dots; subcut into two 6" C squares and a variety of 2"–3½"-wide B strips.

7. Cut five 2¼" by fabric width strips from yellow polka dots for binding.

8. Cut (50) 4" squares fabric stabilizer.

Preparing the Appliqué Circles

1. Prepare templates for the circles using the templates given on page 97.

2. Trace circle shapes onto the paper side of the fusible web as directed on each pattern for number to cut; cut out shapes, leaving a margin around each one.

3. Fuse shapes to the wrong side of fabrics as directed on patterns; cut out shapes on traced lines. Remove paper backing.

Completing the Circle Blocks

1. Fold each A square in half vertically and horizontally and crease to mark the centers. Repeat with each large circle.

2. Randomly select an A square and a large circle (not the same fabric); center and fuse the large circle to the A square.

3. Repeat step 2 with all A squares and large circles.

4. Pin a 4" stabilizer square to the wrong side of each fused block. Using a machine blanket stitch and cream all-purpose thread, stitch around the edge of each circle to complete the blocks; remove fabric stabilizer.

5. Select a small circle and a C square; fuse the circle to the square using random placement. Repeat to make four squares.

6. Repeat step 4 to complete four Corner blocks.

Completing the Quilt Top

1. Arrange and join the Circle blocks in six rows of five blocks each, placing colors diagonally from top to bottom as shown in the Placement Diagram; press seams in adjacent rows in opposite directions.

2. Join the rows to complete the pieced center; press seams in one direction.

3. Join the B strips in peach-yellow-green-pink-blue order along the 6" sides to make a strip at least 145" long; press seams in one direction. Trim strip to make two 39½" E borders and two 33" F borders.

4. Referring to the Placement Diagram, randomly place and fuse remaining small circles to E and F strips. Repeat step 4 of Completing the Circle Blocks for each circle.

5. Sew E borders to opposite long sides of the pieced center; press seams toward E borders.

6. Sew a Corner block to each end of each F border; press seams toward F borders.

7. Sew the F/Corner borders to the top and bottom of the pieced center to complete the pieced top; press seams toward F/Corner borders.

Completing the Quilt

1. Press quilt top on both sides; check for proper seam pressing and trim all loose threads.

2. Sandwich batting between the stitched top and the prepared backing piece; pin or baste layers together to hold. Quilt on marked lines and as desired by hand or machine.

3. When quilting is complete, remove pins or basting. Trim batting and backing fabric edges even with raw edges of quilt top.

4. Join binding strips on short ends with diagonal seams to make one long strip; trim seams to ¼" and press seams open.

5. Fold the binding strip in half with wrong sides together along length; press.

6. Sew binding to quilt edges, matching raw edges, mitering corners and overlapping ends.

7. Fold binding to the back side and stitch in place to finish. ■

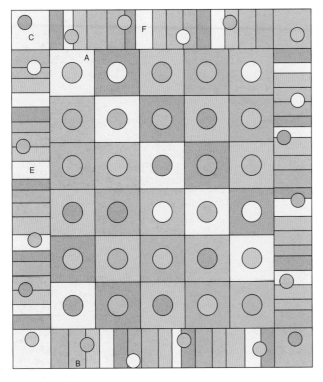

Dots Done Your Way
Placement Diagram 43½" x 50"

Small Circle
Cut 4 each polka-dot fabric

Large Circle
Cut 6 each polka-dot fabric

Black Lily Bag

Stitch up a stylish, quilted bag using a dramatic combination of black and white.

DESIGN BY SUE KIM

PROJECT SPECIFICATIONS

Skill Level: Intermediate
Bag Size: 12½" x 8" x 3"

MATERIALS

- ⅛ yard black eyelet
- ¼ yard black-with-white print
- ¼ yard white-with-black print
- ½ yard black solid
- ⅝ yard white print
- Batting: 2 (10" x 14") and 1 (3½" x 29") pieces
- Black all-purpose thread
- Clear nylon thread
- 7 white pearl beads
- ½" silver magnetic clasp
- 5" x 8¼" black handle set
- Basic sewing tools and supplies

Cutting

1. Prepare small and large flower templates from patterns provided. Cut four Small Flowers from black eyelet.

2. Cut three 1¾" by fabric width strips from black-with-white print. Subcut into (10) 1¾" x 8½" B strips.

3. Cut three 1¾" by fabric width strips from white-with-black print. Subcut into (10) 1¾" x 8½" A strips.

4. Cut one 3½" by fabric width strip from black solid; subcut into one 3½" x 29" C strip.

5. Cut one 2" by fabric width strip from black solid; subcut into four 2" x 5" D pieces.

6. Cut one 1½" by fabric width strip from black solid for binding.

7. Cut four Large Flowers, using prepared template from step 1, from black solid remnants.

8. Cut one 10" by fabric width strip from white print; subcut into two 10" x 14" A/B lining rectangles.

9. Cut two 1½" by fabric width binding strips and one 3½" x 29" C lining strip from white print.

Assembly

1. Lay an A/B lining rectangle on a flat surface; place a 10" x 14" batting piece on top.

2. Lay an A piece right side up onto the layered batting and lining as shown in Figure 1; place a B piece right sides together with A and stitch along one long edge, again referring to Figure 1.

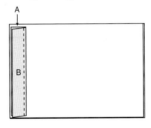

Figure 1

3. Press piece B to the right side. Continue adding A and B pieces alternately until you have used five of each piece to complete a patchwork rectangle as shown in Figure 2; repeat to make two patchwork rectangles.

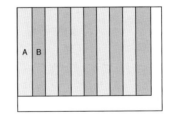

Figure 2

4. Trim the lining and batting rectangles even with patchwork edges to make two 8½" x 13" rectangles.

5. Designate one 13" edge as the top on each patchwork rectangle; mark in ½" on each top end as shown in Figure 3.

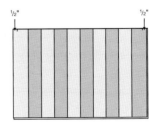

Figure 3

6. Using a straightedge, cut from the bottom corner to the marked line on each top edge end to make angled ends as shown in Figure 4.

Figure 4

7. Sandwich the 3½" x 29" batting strip between the C and C lining pieces; baste layers together at edges to hold.

8. Prepare a trimming template using the pattern given. Place the template on each end of the layered C strip and trim to make angled ends as shown in Figure 5.

Figure 5

9. Pin the layered C piece right sides together with one of the A-B patchwork pieces starting on one top edge and ending on the opposite top edge. Stitch, stopping at corner seam allowance and pivoting to turn the corner as shown in Figure 6. Clip corners a little to ease the layered C piece around the corner.

Figure 6

10. Repeat step 9 with the second A-B patchwork piece on the opposite edge of C to complete the bag shell.

11. Fold ¼" to the wrong sides on one long raw edge of the lining binding strips; press.

12. Pin and stitch the raw edge of one binding strip right sides together with the A-B-C unit, stitching as shown in Figure 7; turn the binding over to encase the seam allowance and hand-stitch in place. Repeat on the remaining A-B-C edge.

A/B   C

Figure 7

13. Repeat step 11 with the black solid binding strip.

14. Pin and stitch the raw edge of the strip along the right side raw edge of the bag top, overlapping beginning and end, trimming excess as needed; turn the strip to the inside and hand-stitch in place to finish the top edge.

15. Fold in each long edge of each D strip to the center of the wrong side as shown in Figure 8; press. Fold in half to complete one handle tab, again referring to Figure 8; repeat to make four handle tabs.

Figure 8

16. Thread a handle tab through the opening in each end of each handle; fold raw ends in ½" and hand- or machine-stitch across bottom of tabs to hem.

17. Measure and place a pin 1¾" down from top inside edge and 2" in from side edge bound seam as shown in Figure 9; place the handle tabs at the pins. Hand-stitch across tabs at base of handle and at bottom of tabs to hold.

Figure 9

18. Hand-stitch magnetic clasp pieces 1" down from the top on the inside center of the bag front and back.

19. Fold each small and large flower shape in half; press.

20. Lay one folded large flower on a flat surface; lay a second large flower to cover half of flower 1 as shown in Figure 10. Lay a third flower to cover half of flower 2, again referring to Figure 10. Place the final folded large flower over half of flower 3 and under flower 1, again referring to Figure 10; secure layers together with pins.

Figure 10

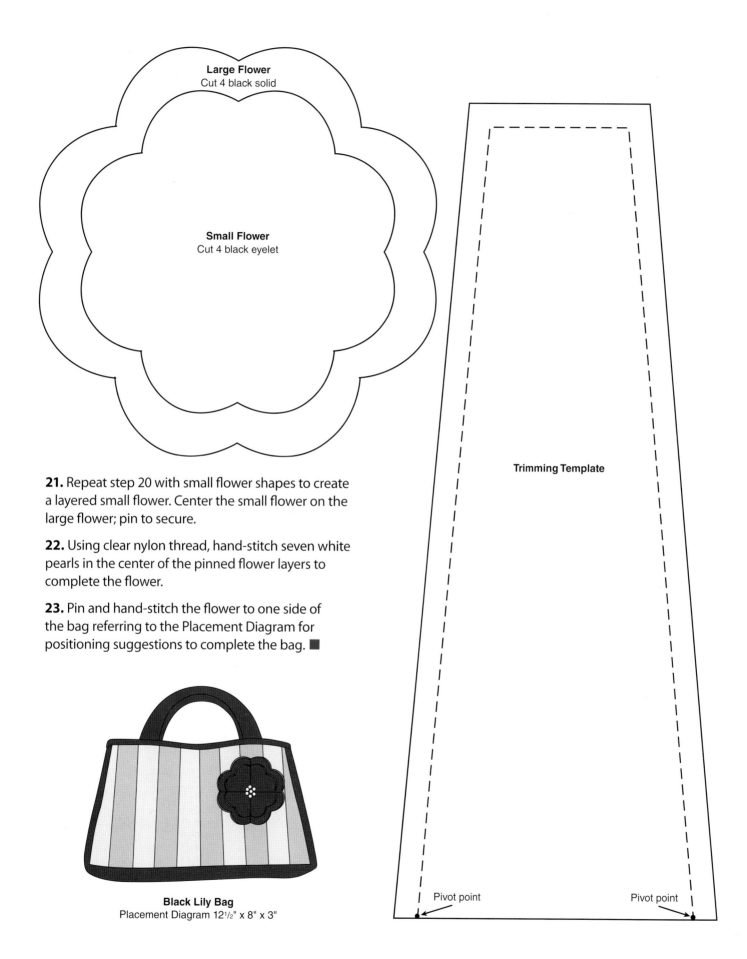

Large Flower
Cut 4 black solid

Small Flower
Cut 4 black eyelet

Trimming Template

21. Repeat step 20 with small flower shapes to create a layered small flower. Center the small flower on the large flower; pin to secure.

22. Using clear nylon thread, hand-stitch seven white pearls in the center of the pinned flower layers to complete the flower.

23. Pin and hand-stitch the flower to one side of the bag referring to the Placement Diagram for positioning suggestions to complete the bag. ▧

Black Lily Bag
Placement Diagram 12¹/₂" x 8" x 3"

Pivot point

Pivot point

E-Reader Tech Bag

Carry your e-reader in style. This sassy bag will become every teen's favorite.

DESIGN BY JILL REBER

PROJECT SPECIFICATIONS

Skill Level: Beginner
Size: 9" x 11"

MATERIALS

- ½ yard print batik
- ¾ yard coordinating solid batik
- Batting 21" x 13"
- Coordinating all-purpose thread
- 2 yards coordinating ½"-wide ribbon, optional
- Fabric basting spray
- Water soluble marking tool
- Basic sewing tools and supplies

Cutting

1. Cut one 12" by fabric width strip form print batik; subcut strip into one 21" x 13" A rectangle.

2. Cut one 13" by fabric width strip from solid batik. Subcut strip into one 13" x 21" B rectangle and one 7" x 13" C rectangle.

3. Cut one 3" by fabric width D strip from solid batik.

4. Cut one 3" by fabric width strip from solid batik; subcut into one 3" x 25" binding strip.

5. Cut ribbon into six 12" lengths.

Completing Bag Body

1. Lay B right side down on flat surface. Layer batting and A, right side up, on B. Follow manufacturer's instructions to spray baste layers together.

2. Quilt as desired using coordinating all-purpose thread.

3. Trim A/B quilted rectangle to 12" x 19" for bag body.

4. Finish all edges with zigzag/overcast stitch or with serger.

5. Using water soluble marking tool, mark on A side of bag body 1¼" from the left short side and 3" from the bottom edge (Figure 1).

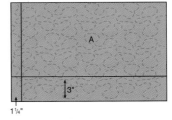

1¼"

Figure 1

6. Mark on A side of bag body, 3½" from top edge and 5" from left short side for pocket ribbon placement (Figure 2).

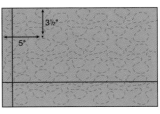

Figure 2

7. Optional: fold a ribbon end back ½". Pin ribbon to bag body at mark with folded edge toward bag and ribbon length toward bag body top (Figure 3).

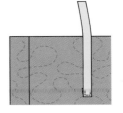

Figure 3

8. Optional: stitch ribbon end to bag body, stitching around edges in a square referring to Figure 3.

Completing the Pocket

1. Fold C in half lengthwise right sides together and stitch ½" side seams, leaving end open referring to Figure 4.

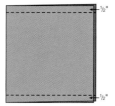

Figure 4

2. Turn right side out and press flat.

3. Finish open end edges with zigzag/overcast stitch or with serger.

4. Mark on wrong side of pocket ¾" from pocket top folded edge and 3" from pocket side (Figure 5).

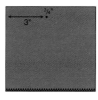

Figure 5

5. Fold ribbon end ½" back. Pin ribbon to pocket at mark with folded edge toward pocket and ribbon length toward pocket top edge. Stitch ribbon to pocket, stitching around edges in a square referring to Figure 3 in Completing Bag Body.

6. Mark a stitching line on pocket wrong side ½" from finished bottom edge of pocket. On right side, mark a stitching line 1" from left side of pocket (Figure 6).

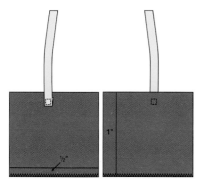

Figure 6

Completing the Strap Handle

1. Press D in half lengthwise wrong sides together.

2. Fold and press again in thirds lengthwise, folding the folded edge over raw edges as shown in Figure 7.

Figure 7

3. Edgestitch along folded center edge with a straight or decorative stitch to make Strap Handle (Figure 8).

Figure 8

4. Trim Strap Handle length to 40", trimming off selveges.

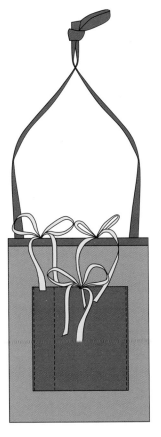

E-Reader Tech Bag
Placement Diagram 9" x 11"

Completing the E-Reader Tech Bag

1. Position and pin pocket bottom to bag body right sides together along pocket position line referring to Figure 9.

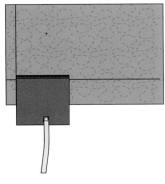

Figure 9

2. Stitch along marked ½" seam line, backstitch to secure seam being sure to keep ribbon away from seam. Press pocket over seam and pin pocket sides to bag body (Figure 10).

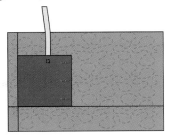

Figure 10

3. Edgestitch pocket sides to bag body, backstitching to secure. Stitch along marked line, backstitching to secure, to make a stylus pocket. **Note:** *To keep pocket ribbons out to the way during construction, place them inside the pocket.*

4. Pin and baste ribbons to top edge of bag body on B side 3", 6½", 12" and 15½" from right side (Figure 11). Pin and baste ends of Strap Handle 8" and 17" from right side, again referring to Figure 11.

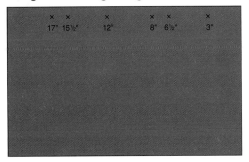

Figure 11

5. Fold bag body in half matching 12" sides with B side out. Stitch ½" seams along sides and bottom of bag body, keeping ribbons and Strap Handle out of the seams (Figure 12).

½"

Figure 12

6. Turn right side out, putting ribbons and Strap Handle inside bag.

7. Fold one short end of 3" x 25" binding strip to wrong side ½" and press. Fold and press binding strip in half, wrong sides together.

8. Beginning with folded short end, pin binding strip to bag top matching raw edges. If necessary, trim strip end and tuck approximately 1" inside folded short edge. Stitch ½" from raw edges.

9. Fold binding to right side of bag and pin over stitching line. Stitch in place with straight or decorative stitch.

10. Pull Strap Handle up and tack ends to binding to complete. ◼

3-D Drunkard's Path Quilt

There are no curved seams to piece when you use this simple method to make an old favorite.

DESIGN BY LUCY FAZELY

PROJECT SPECIFICATIONS

Skill Level: Beginner
Quilt Size: 45½" x 61½"
Block Size: 4" x 4"
Number of Blocks: 140

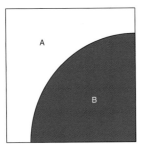

3-D Drunkard's Path
4" x 4" Block
Make 140

MATERIALS

- 1 fat quarter each 4 red prints
- 1 fat quarter each 5 different orange, yellow, green, blue, indigo and violet prints
- ⅜ yard each 9 different white tonals
- 1¼ yards red print 5
- Batting 54" x 70"
- Backing 54" x 70"
- Neutral-color all-purpose thread
- Quilting thread
- Basic sewing tools and supplies

Cutting

1. Cut two 4½" by fabric width strips from each white tonal; subcut strips into a total of (140) 4½" A squares.

2. Cut two 3¼" x 40½" C strips red print 5.

3. Cut three 3¼" by fabric width D strips red print 5.

4. Cut six 2¼" by fabric width strips red print 5 for binding.

5. Cut one 7½" by fabric width strip from the remaining red print 5; subcut strip into two 7½" B squares.

6. Cut one 7½" x 21" strip from each of the four additional red prints and each orange, yellow, green, blue, indigo and violet print. Subcut each strip into two 7½" B squares. **Note:** *You should now have 35 matching pairs of B squares.*

Completing the Blocks

1. Fold one B square in each matching set vertically and horizontally and crease to mark the centers.

2. Prepare a template for the circle using pattern given. Trace a circle onto the wrong side of the creased square using the circle template and referring to Figure 1.

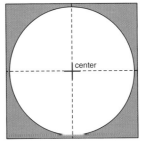

Figure 1

3. Place a marked B square right sides together with a matching color B square; pin layers together to secure.

4. Stitch around each traced circle on the marked line; cut the stitched circles into quarters on the creased lines as shown in Figure 2.

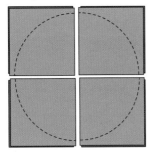

Figure 2

5. Trim excess beyond stitched line on each unit to ¼" as shown in Figure 3.

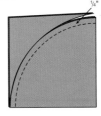

Figure 3

3-D Drunkard's Path Quilt
Placement Diagram 45½" x 61½"

6. Clip curves and turn each stitched unit right side out and press the curved edges flat to complete a total of four B units as shown in Figure 4.

Figure 4

7. Repeat steps 3–5 with the remaining B squares to make a total of 140 B units.

8. Pin a B unit to one corner of an A square, matching corner edges as shown in Figure 5; machine-baste B to A at corners using a ⅛" seam allowance to complete one 3-D Drunkard's Path block, again referring to Figure 5.

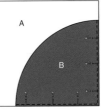

Figure 5

9. Repeat step 8 to complete a total of 140 3-D Drunkard's Path blocks.

Completing the Quilt

1. On a large flat surface, arrange the blocks in 14 rows of 10 blocks each, turning every other block and making diagonal rows shades of the same color referring to the Placement Diagram.

2. When satisfied with the arrangement, join blocks in rows. Press seams in adjoining rows in opposite directions.

3. Join the rows as stitched to complete the pieced center; press seams in one direction.

4. Sew a C strip to the top and bottom of the pieced center; press seams toward C strips.

5. Join the D strips on short ends to make a long strip; press seams open. Subcut the strip into two 62" D strips.

6. Sew a D strip to opposite long sides of the pieced center; press seams toward C and D strips.

7. Press quilt top on both sides; check for proper seam pressing and trim all loose threads.

8. Sandwich batting between the stitched top and the prepared backing piece; pin or baste layers together to hold. Quilt as desired by hand or machine. ***Note:*** *Do not quilt through the layered B pieces.*

9. When quilting is complete, remove pins or basting. Trim batting and backing edges fabric even with raw edges of quilt top.

10. Join binding strips on short ends with diagonal seams to make one long strip; trim seams to ¼" and press seams open.

11. Fold the binding strip in half with wrong sides together along length; press.

12. Sew binding to quilt edges, matching raw edges, mitering corners and overlapping ends.

13. Fold binding to the back side and stitch in place to finish. ■

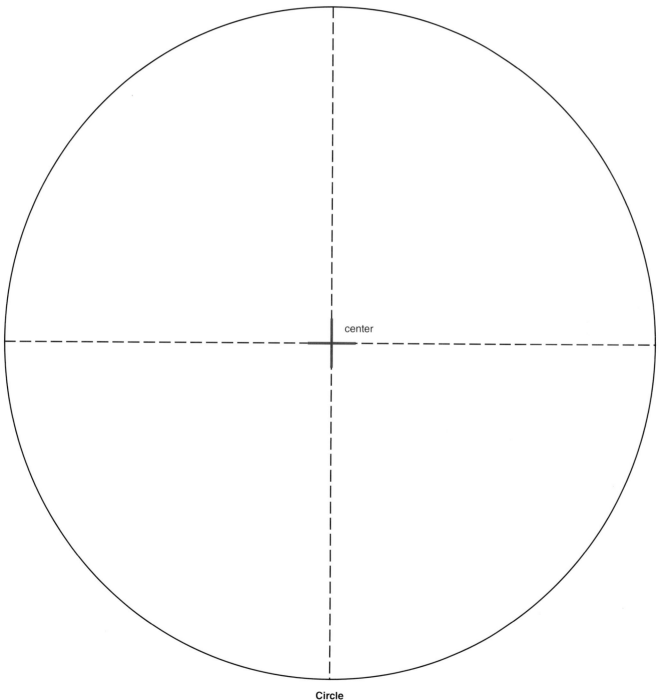

center

Circle
Trace as per instructions

Log Cabin Doll Quilt

Wouldn't you love to snuggle with your favorite doll in this cozy and quick quilt?

DESIGN BY JODI G. WARNER

PROJECT SPECIFICATIONS

Skill Level: Beginner
Quilt Size: 20" x 24"
Block Size: 4" x 4"
Number of Blocks: 20

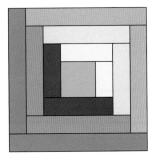

Log Cabin
4" x 4" Block
Make 20

MATERIALS

- Assorted scraps gold, red and blue prints or plaids
- Assorted scraps cream prints or stripes
- ¼ yard red tonal
- ⅓ yard dark blue print
- ⅓ yard medium blue solid
- Batting 28" x 32"
- Backing 28" x 32"
- Neutral-color all-purpose thread
- Quilting thread
- Thin paper
- Basic sewing tools and supplies

Cutting

1. Cut (20) 1½" x 1½" squares from assorted gold scraps for piece 1.

2. Cut the red, blue, gold and cream scraps into 1¼"-wide strips.

3. Cut two 1" x 16½" A strips and two 1" x 21½" B strips red tonal.

4. Cut two 2" x 17½" C strips and two 2" x 24½" D strips dark blue tonal.

5. Cut three 2¼" by fabric width strips medium blue print for binding.

Completing the Blocks

1. Prepare 20 copies of the Log Cabin paper-piecing pattern.

2. Select one paper foundation and a gold piece 1 square; turn paper to the unmarked side and pin piece 1 on the space marked 1 on the opposite side. Measure the length of piece 2 and cut a 1¼"-wide cream scrap strip this length plus ½". Pin piece 2 right sides together with piece 1 on the side with the lines between pieces 1 and 2 as shown in Figure 1.

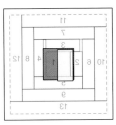

Figure 1

3. Turn the paper over and stitch on the line between pieces 1 and 2, taking at least one stitch before the beginning of the line and at the end as shown in Figure 2.

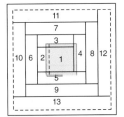

Figure 2

4. Turn the paper over, press piece 2 to the right side as shown in Figure 3.

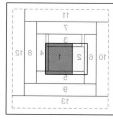 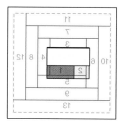

Figure 3   Figure 4

5. Repeat steps 1–4 with piece 3 on pieces 1 and 2 as shown in Figure 4.

6. Repeat steps 1–5 with all pieces referring to pattern for color placement; trim outer edges even with outer line on paper pattern to complete one Log Cabin block. Remove paper backing.

7. Repeat steps 1–6 to complete a total of 20 Log Cabin blocks.

Completing the Quilt

1. Select and join four Log Cabin blocks to make a row as shown in Figure 5; press seams in one direction. Repeat to make a total of five rows, pressings seams in two rows in one direction and three rows in the opposite direction.

Figure 5

2. Arrange and join the rows with seams in adjoining rows facing in opposite directions to complete the pieced center; press seams in one direction.

3. Sew an A strip to the top and bottom and B strips to opposite long sides of the pieced center; press seams toward A and B strips.

Log Cabin Doll Quilt
Placement Diagram 20" x 24"

4. Sew a C strip to the top and bottom and D strips to opposite long sides of the pieced center; press seams toward C and D strips to complete the pieced top.

5. Mark quilting lines through both diagonals of each Log Cabin block and a ¼" echo line beyond the seams of the outer borders.

6. Press quilt top on both sides; check for proper seam pressing and trim all loose threads.

7. Sandwich batting between the stitched top and the prepared backing piece; pin or baste layers together to hold. Quilt on marked lines and as desired by hand or machine.

8. When quilting is complete, remove pins or basting. Trim batting and backing fabric even with raw edges of quilt top.

9. Join binding strips on short ends with diagonal seams to make one long strip; trim seams to ¼" and press seams open.

10. Fold the binding strip in half with wrong sides together along length; press.

11. Sew binding to quilt edges, matching raw edges, mitering corners and overlapping ends.

12. Fold binding to the back side and stitch in place to finish. ■

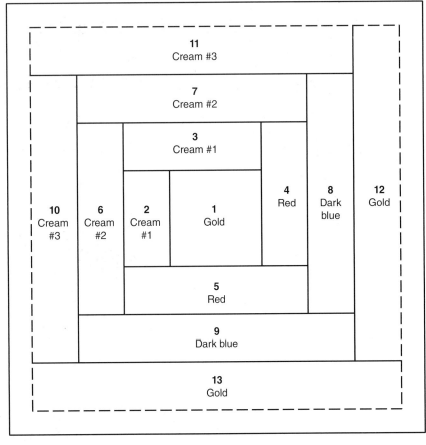

Log Cabin Paper-Piecing Pattern
Make 20 copies

24-Hour Treasures

Combine your love of mixing colors and these great projects and you are sure to come up with a winner every time! Quilt the Sleepytime Lambs Baby Quilt for a new arrival into the family, or complete the Friendship Stars Backpack to give as a wonderful gift. Dig into your stash or scraps and quilt the Twisted Rail Fence or Magic Maze. You'll be amazed at how wonderfully different each project looks using your special fabrics.

Batiks Squared

It's time to put a dent in your batik stash. This quilt does the trick.

DESIGN BY JILL REBER
QUILTED BY DARLENE GLIDEWELL

PROJECT SPECIFICATIONS

Skill Level: Beginner
Quilt Size: 74" x 98"
Block Size: 6" x 6"
Number of Blocks: 64

Batik Five-Patch
6" x 6" Block
Make 64

MATERIALS

- ⅝ yard each 8 batiks
- 1¾ yards dark-colored batik
- 2⅝ yards print batik
- Backing 82" x 106"
- Batting 82" x 106"
- Neutral-color all-purpose thread
- Quilting thread
- Basic sewing tools and supplies

Cutting

1. Cut five 2½" by fabric width A, B, E, F and H strips from each of the 8 batiks.

2. Subcut A into one 2½" x 21" strip.

3. Subcut each E strip into (12) 2½" x 4½" E rectangles for a total of 96 rectangles.

4. Subcut each F strip into (12) 2½" F squares for a total of 96 squares.

5. Subcut each H strip into five 2½" H squares. Discard five for a total of 35 squares.

6. Cut one 6½" by fabric width strip from each of 8 batiks. Subcut each strip into (12) 2½" x 6½" C rectangles for a total of 128 rectangles.

7. Cut six 2½" by fabric width strips from dark-colored batik. Subcut into (96) 2½" D squares.

8. Cut four 10½" by fabric width strips from dark-colored batik. Subcut into (58) 2½" x 10½" G rectangles.

9. Cut six 6½" by fabric width I/J strips from print batik.

10. Cut two 6½" x 26½" L strips and two 6½" x 38½" K strips from print batik.

11. Cut nine 2¼" by fabric width strips from print batik for binding.

Completing the Blocks

1. Select one 2½" x 21" A strip. Cut one B strip to make two 2½" x 21" B strips.

2. Sew the A strip between the two B strips to make an A-B strip; press seams toward B strips.

3. Subcut the A-B strip into one set of eight 2½" A-B units as shown in Figure 1.

Figure 1

4. Repeat steps 1–3 to make eight different A-B sets.

5. To complete one matching set of eight Batik Five-Patch blocks, select one set of eight matching A-B units and 16 C rectangles from the same fabric as B.

6. Sew a C rectangle to opposite sides of each A-B unit to complete eight matching blocks; press seams toward C rectangles.

5. Sew a D square between two E rectangles to make a D-E unit as shown in Figure 4; press seams toward E rectangles. Repeat to make two D-E units.

Figure 4

6. Sew a D-E unit to the remaining sides of the Batik Five-Patch block to complete a block unit as shown in Figure 5; press seams toward D-E units.

Figure 5

7. Repeat steps 2–6 to complete 24 block units.

8. Join four block units with five G strips to make a block row, sewing G to the D-F sides of the blocks as shown in Figure 6; press seams toward G strips. Repeat to make six block rows.

Figure 6

9. Join four G strips with five H squares to make a sashing row as shown in Figure 7; press seams toward G strips. Repeat to make seven sashing rows.

Make 7

Figure 7

10. Join the block rows with the sashing rows, beginning and ending with sashing rows; press seams toward sashing rows to complete the pieced center.

Completing the Quilt

1. Join the I/J strips on short ends to make one long strip; press seams open. Subcut strips into two 62½" I strips and two 50½" J strips.

7. Repeat steps 1–6 to complete eight sets of matching blocks to total 64 blocks.

Completing the Pieced Center

1. Select and set aside 40 Batik Five-Patch blocks for borders.

2. Select four each E rectangles and F squares from one fabric and four D squares from another fabric.

3. Sew a D square between two F squares to make a D-F unit as shown in Figure 2; press seams toward F squares. Repeat to make two D-F units.

Figure 2

4. Sew a D-F unit to the C sides of one Batik Five-Patch block as shown in Figure 3; press seams toward C.

Figure 3

2. Sew the B side of one Batik Five-Patch block to each end of each I strip as shown in Figure 8; press seams toward I strips. Repeat to make two I/block strips.

Figure 8

3. Repeat step 1 with two Batik Five-Patch blocks on each end of each J strip to make two J/block strips, again referring to Figure 8.

4. Join one each I/block strip and J/block strip along length to make a side strip; press seams toward I/block strip. Repeat to make two side strips.

5. Sew a side strip to opposite long sides of the pieced center referring to the Placement Diagram for positioning; press seams toward side strips.

6. Join three blocks on the C sides; press seams in one direction. Repeat to make two three-block units and two four-block units as shown in Figure 9.

Figure 9

7. Sew a three-block unit to each end of each K strip and a four-block unit to each end of each L strip to make two each K/block and L/block strips as shown in Figure 10; press seams toward strips.

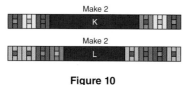

Figure 10

8. Join one each K/block strip and L/block strip to make the top strip as shown in Figure 11; press seam toward the L/block strip. Repeat to make the bottom strip.

Figure 11

9. Sew the top and bottom strips to the top and bottom of the pieced top referring to the Placement Diagram to complete the pieced top; press seams toward strips.

Completing the Quilt

1. Press quilt top on both sides; check for proper seam pressing and trim all loose threads.

2. Sandwich batting between the stitched top and the prepared backing piece; pin or baste layers together to hold. Quilt on marked lines and as desired by hand or machine.

3. When quilting is complete, remove pins or basting. Trim batting and backing fabric edges even with raw edges of quilt top.

4. Join binding strips on short ends with diagonal seams to make one long strip; trim seams to ¼" and press seams open.

5. Fold the binding strip in half with wrong sides together along length; press.

6. Sew binding to quilt edges, matching raw edges, mitering corners and overlapping ends.

7. Fold binding to the back side and stitch in place to finish. ■

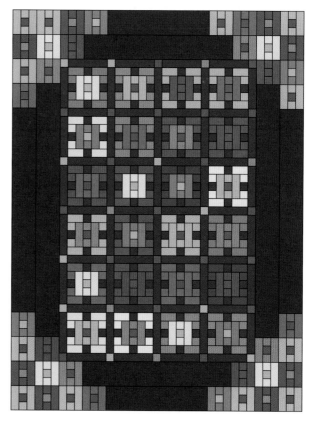

Batiks Squared
Placement Diagram 74" x 98"

Button Checkerboard

Take your family back to the simple, good old days with the rustic colors and Bear Paw borders of this checkerboard. This is a perfect addition to a porch or family room.

DESIGN BY CHRIS MALONE

PROJECT SPECIFICATIONS

Skill Level: Confident Beginner
Project Size: 19½" x 12"
Block Size: 3" x 3"
Number of Blocks: 8

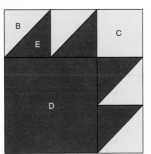

Bear Paw
3" x 3" Block
Make 8

MATERIALS

- 1 fat quarter brown/black print
- 1 fat quarter tan print
- 1 (5") square each green, gold, rust and blue prints
- ¼ yard solid black
- Backing 16" x 22"
- Batting 16" x 22"
- 8 (⁹⁄₁₆") black buttons
- 6 light-color buttons or wooden circles
- 6 dark-color buttons or wooden circles
- ½ yard ecru cord or size 5 pearl cotton
- Neutral-color all-purpose thread
- Quilting thread
- Basic sewing tools and supplies

Cutting

1. Cut three 2" x 22" A strips brown/black print.

2. Cut one 6½" x 8½" rectangle for checkers storage bag from brown/black print.

3. Cut five 2" x 21" B strips tan print; subcut two strips into (16) 2" B squares.

4. Cut one 1½" x 21" strip tan print; subcut strip into eight 1½" C squares.

5. From each green, gold, rust and blue print scrap, cut two 2½" D squares and four 2" E squares.

6. Cut one 1¼" by fabric width strip solid black; subcut strip into two 12½" F strips.

7. Cut two 2¼" by fabric width strips solid black for binding.

Completing Checkerboard

1. Stitch an A strip to a B strip to make an A-B strip set. Press seam toward strip A. Repeat to make three strip sets.

2. Cut each strip set into (32) 2" A-B units (Figure 1).

Figure 1

3. Referring to Figure 2, join eight A-B units, reversing every other unit, to make a row. Repeat to make four rows. Press seams in two rows to the left and in two rows to the right.

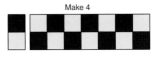

Figure 2

4. Join rows to complete the checkerboard center as shown in Figure 3, with seams pressed in opposite directions in each row. Press seams in one direction.

Figure 3

5. Sew F border strips to opposite sides of checkerboard center. Press seams toward F.

Completing the Bear Paw Blocks

1. Draw a diagonal line from corner to corner on wrong side of each 2" B square.

2. Layer an E square right sides together with B and stitch ¼" on each side of marked line (Figure 4). Cut apart on the marked line and press seams toward E to complete a B-E unit.

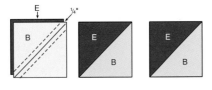

Figure 4

Button Checkerboard
Placement Diagram 19½" x 12"

3. Trim square to 1½" x 1½" aligning 45-degree line of ruler with seam on the B-E unit as shown in Figure 5.

Figure 5

4. Repeat steps 2 and 3 with same-color E square to make four matching B-E units.

5. Join two B-E units; press seam in direction of arrow (Figure 6).

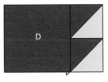

Figure 6

6. Sew stitched B-E units to one side of a matching D square (Figure 7). Press seam toward D.

Figure 7

7. Join remaining two B-E units and a C square referring to Figure 8. Press seams toward C.

Figure 8

8. Join the B-E-C and the B-E-D units referring to Figure 9 to make a Bear Paw block. Repeat steps 2–7 to make two Bear Paw blocks each using green, gold, rust and blue prints.

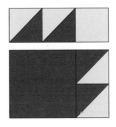

Figure 9

Completing the Checkerboard

1. Join four Bear Paw blocks to make a row using one of each color and referring to the Placement Diagram. Repeat to make a second row.

2. Sew a row to each F side of the checkerboard center, reversing the direction of the rows to complete the pieced top as shown in the Placement Diagram. Press seams toward F.

3. Press the pieced top on both sides; check for proper seam pressing and trim all loose threads.

4. Sandwich batting between the stitched top and the prepared backing piece; pin or baste layers together to hold. Quilt as desired by hand or machine.

5. When quilting is complete, remove pins or basting. Trim batting and backing fabric edges even with raw edges of quilt top.

6. Join binding strips on short ends with diagonal seams to make one long strip; trim seams to ¼" and press seams open.

7. Fold the binding strip in half with wrong sides together along length; press.

8. Sew binding to quilt edges, matching raw edges, mitering corners and overlapping ends.

9. Fold binding to the back side and stitch in place.

10. Sew a black button to the center of each Bear Paw block to finish.

Completing the Checkers Storage Bag

1. To make a storage bag for checkers, turn and press ¼" to wrong side of the 6½" edge of 6½" x 8½" brown/black rectangle. Turn and press ¼" to wrong side again and edgestitch to make a double-turned hem.

2. Fold the rectangle in half right sides together and matching raw edges. Sew along raw-edge sides and bottom. Trim corners and turn right side out.

3. For drawstring, use cord or pearl cotton and sew a gathering stitch 1" down from hemmed top, starting and ending stitching at center front. Tie a knot at each end of thread.

4. For checkers, use 12 dark and 12 light ¾" buttons or purchased wooden circles painted or stained to coordinate with fabrics. ■

Twisted Rail Fence

Add a twist to the simple Rail Fence pattern with this contemporary variation.

DESIGN BY MARY WILBUR

PATTERN SPECIFICATIONS

Skill Level: Intermediate
Quilt Size: 46½" x 66½"
Block Size: 15" x 15"
Number of Blocks: 9

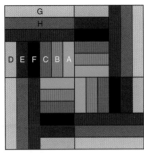

Twisted Rail Fence
15" x 15" Block
Make 9

MATERIALS

- ¼ yard lightest teal print
- ½ yard total dark teal solids/tonals
- ½ yard total light teal solids/tonals
- ½ yard total light purple prints
- ½ yard total dark purple prints
- ½ yard total light pink solids/tonals/prints
- ½ yard total medium pink solids/tonals/prints
- ⅔ yard dark pink tonals
- ⅞ yard solid black
- ⅞ yard total medium teal solids/tonals
- Backing 53" x 73"
- Batting 53" x 73"
- Neutral-color all-purpose thread
- Quilting thread
- Basic sewing tools and supplies

Cutting

1. Cut two 1⅝" by fabric width strips from lightest teal print; subcut strips into (12) 1⅝" x 6" O strips.

2. Cut one 1¾" by fabric width A strip from lightest teal print.

3. Cut five 1¾" by fabric width C strips and two 1⅝" by fabric width L strips from variety dark teal solids/tonals.

4. Cut four 1¾" by fabric width A strips and two 1⅝" by fabric width J strips from variety light teal solids/tonals.

5. Cut four 1¾" by fabric width D strips and three 1⅝" by fabric width T strips from variety light purple prints.

6. Cut four 1¾" by fabric width E strips and two 1⅝" by fabric width N strips from variety dark purple prints.

7. Cut eight 1¾" by fabric width G strips from variety light pink solids/tonals/prints.

8. Cut eight 1¾" by fabric width H strips from variety medium pink solids/tonals/prints.

9. Cut eight 1¾" by fabric width I strips and three 1⅝" by fabric width S strips from dark pink mottled.

10. Cut four 1¾" by fabric width F strips, two 1⅝" by fabric width M strips, three 1⅝" by fabric width Q strips and three 1⅝" by fabric width R strips from solid black.

11. Cut five 1¾" by fabric width B strips, two 1⅝" by fabric width K strips, three 1⅝" by fabric width P strips and three 1¾" by fabric width U strips from variety medium teal solids/tonals.

Completing the Blocks

1. Join one each A, B and C strip with right sides together along the length to make an A-B-C strip set; press seams from light to dark. Repeat to make five A-B-C strip sets.

2. Subcut the A-B-C strip sets into nine sets of four matching 4¼" A units as shown in Figure 1.

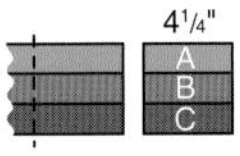

Figure 1

3. Join one each D, E and F strip with right sides together along the length to make a D-E-F strip set; press seams from dark to light. Repeat to make four D-E-F strip sets.

4. Subcut the D-E-F strip sets into nine sets of four matching 4¼" D units as shown in Figure 2.

Figure 2

5. Join one each G, H and I strip with right sides together along the length to make a G-H-I strip set; press seams from light to dark. Repeat to make eight G-H-I strip sets.

6. Subcut the G-H-I strip sets into nine sets of four matching 8" G units as shown in Figure 3.

Figure 3

7. To complete one Twisted Rail Fence block, select four each matching A, matching D and matching G units; join one A unit with one D unit as shown in Figure 4. Repeat to make four A-D units; press seams toward the A units.

Make 4

Figure 4

8. Sew an A-D unit to a G unit to complete a block quarter as shown in Figure 5; press seam toward the G unit. Repeat to make four block quarters.

Make 4

Figure 5

9. Join two block quarters to make a row as shown in Figure 6; press seam in one direction. Repeat to make two rows.

Make 2

Figure 6

10. Join the rows to complete one Twisted Rail Fence block referring to the block drawing; press seam in one direction. Repeat to make nine blocks.

Completing the Quilt

1. Arrange and join three blocks to make a row; repeat to make three rows. Press seams in one direction.

2. Join the rows to complete the pieced center; press seams in one direction.

3. Join one each J, K, L, M and N strip with right sides together along the length to make a J-K-L-M-N strip set; press seams in one direction. Repeat to make two strip sets.

4. Subcut the J-K-L-M-N strip sets into (14) 6" J units as shown in Figure 7.

Figure 7

Twisted Rail Fence
Placement Diagram 46½" x 66½"

5. Join seven J units with six O strips to make a J-O strip as shown in Figure 8; press seams in one direction. Repeat to make two J-O strips. Trim strips evenly on both ends to make 45½"-long strips.

Figure 8

6. Sew a J-O strip to the top and bottom of the pieced center; press seams toward the J-O strips.

7. Join the P strips on short ends to make one long strip; press seams open. Subcut strip into two 45½" P strips. Repeat with Q strips to make two 45½" Q strips.

8. Sew a P strip to a Q strip with right sides together along length; repeat to make two P-Q strips. Press seams toward Q strips.

9. Sew a P-Q strip to the top and bottom of the pieced center referring to the Placement Diagram for positioning; press seams toward P-Q strips.

10. Join the R strips on the short ends to make one long strip; press seams open. Subcut strip into two 61" R strips.

11. Sew an R strip to opposite long sides of the pieced center; press seams toward R strips.

12. Repeat step 7 with S, T and U strips; subcut strips to make two 47½" strips each S, T and U.

13. Sew an S strip to a T strip to a U strip with right sides together along the length; press seams in one direction. Repeat to make two S-T-U strips.

14. Sew an S-T-U strip to the top and bottom of the pieced center referring to the Placement Diagram for positioning to complete the pieced top; press seams toward the S-T-U strips.

15. Sandwich the batting between the completed top and the prepared backing piece; pin or baste to hold.

16. Quilt as desired by hand or machine, stopping stitching 1" from edge all around; remove pins or basting.

17. Trim the backing and batting ¾" smaller than quilt top all around.

18. Turn under the outside edge of the top ¼"; press. Turn the folded edge to the back side and hand- or machine-stitch in place to finish the edges. ■

Sleepytime Lambs Baby Quilt

Warm, fuzzy lambs are a perfect sleep aid for tiny tots.

DESIGN BY BARBARA CLAYTON

PROJECT SPECIFICATIONS

Skill Level: Beginner
Quilt Size: 39" x 50"
Block Size: 7" x 7"
Number of Blocks: 4

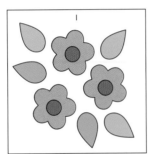

Flower Corner
7" x 7" Block
Make 4

MATERIALS

- Scraps light, medium and bright pink
- Scraps light and medium green
- ⅜ yard white imitation lamb's wool fabric
- ⅜ yard medium pink print
- ⅔ yard dark pink solid fabric for sashing and appliqué
- 1¼ yards white solid fabric
- 1⅓ yards pink-and-white stripe with stripe running along the length of the fabric
- Backing 47" x 58"
- Low loft batting 47" x 58"
- All-purpose thread to blend with appliqué fabrics
- Black and white all-purpose thread
- Dark pink quilting thread
- Clear nylon monofilament thread
- 1 yard medium-weight fusible interfacing
- Recycled manila folder or cardstock
- Stylus, knitting needle or pencil with no lead
- Basic sewing tools and supplies

Cutting

1. Cut two 4½" by fabric width strips each medium pink print (A) and pink-and-white stripe (B); subcut strips into (12) 4" rectangles each fabric.

2. Cut two 7½" x 32½" F strips and two 7½" x 21½" G strips pink-and-white stripe with stripes running vertically.

3. Cut three 4½" by fabric width strips white solid; subcut strips into (24) 4" C rectangles.

4. Cut one 7½" by fabric width strip white solid; subcut strip into four 7½" I squares.

5. Cut five 2½" by fabric width strips white solid for binding.

6. Cut two 1½" x 21½" D strips and two 1½" x 34½" E strips dark pink solid.

7. Cut two 1½" by fabric width strips dark pink solid; subcut strips into eight 7½" H strips.

8. Cut two 1½" x 37½" J strips dark pink solid.

9. Cut three 1½" by fabric width strips dark pink solid. Join strips on the short ends to make one long strip; press seams open. Subcut strip into two 50½" K strips.

Preparing the Appliqué Pieces

1. Trace 24 heart shapes onto the smooth side of the fusible interfacing, leaving ½" between shapes when tracing.

2. Pin the traced interfacing to the right side of the dark pink solid with traced lines up; stitch the interfacing to the fabric on the traced lines as shown in Figure 1.

Figure 1

3. Cut out shapes, leaving a ⅛" seam allowance around each one referring to Figure 2; clip curves and trim points.

Figure 2

4. Cut a small slit in the interfacing side of each heart shape and turn right side out through the opening. With a stylus, knitting needle or pencil, smooth out the edges by running around the seam on the inside.

5. Repeat steps 1–4 with the remaining appliqué shapes (except flower centers) referring to patterns for color and number to cut for each shape. Leave faces, inner ears and legs open for turning rather than slitting the interfacing.

6. Cut the 28 flower centers from dark pink solid using pattern given; cut seven flower center guides from recycled manila folders or cardstock.

7. With a doubled dark pink thread, work a gathering stitch around the right side of one flower center piece; center a cardstock guide on the wrong side of the stitched flower center as shown in Figure 3.

Figure 3

8. Pull the thread tight around the cardstock guide and knot; press the circle flat. Snip gathering thread and remove the guide.

9. Repeat steps 7 and 8 with all flower centers, using new guides as necessary to retain shape.

10. Center a flower center on a flower and machine-stitch in place using clear nylon monofilament and a narrow blind hemstitch.

Appliqué

1. Fold each C rectangle and I square and F and G strip in half vertically and horizontally and crease to mark the centers.

2. Center and fuse a heart shape on a creased C rectangle as shown in Figure 4; repeat with all heart shapes and C rectangles.

Figure 4

3. Center and fuse two each light and medium pink flowers and two medium green and three light green leaf shapes to the center of each F strip referring to Figure 5.

Figure 5

4. Center and fuse a lamb motif on each side of the fused flower/leaf motifs with pieces in numerical order referring to Figure 6.

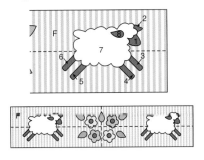

Figure 6

5. Center and fuse a lamb motif on each G strip as in step 4.

6. Center and fuse two medium pink flower motifs, one light green leaf and two dark green leaves on each side of the fused lamb shape on each G strip referring to the Placement Diagram.

7. Center and fuse two each light and medium pink flower motifs on each side of the fused lamb motif on each G strip, again referring to the Placement Diagram for positioning.

8. To fuse pieces for the Flower Corner blocks, arrange and fuse three bright pink flower shapes, two light green and three medium green leaf shapes to each I square referring to Figure 7 for positioning.

Figure 7

9. Using clear nylon monofilament and a narrow blind hemstitch, machine-stitch around the edges of each fused shape to secure.

10. Pin a small piece of paper to the back of each lamb face to stabilize for stitching the eyes. With black thread and referring to Figure 8, work a narrow zigzag to outline the eye, and then fill in with a medium satin stitch to cover the eye area; remove the paper after stitching.

Figure 8

Completing the Quilt

1. Select, arrange and join one B, two A and three fused C heart rectangles to make a W row as shown in Figure 9; press seams away from the fused C heart rectangles. Repeat to make two W rows.

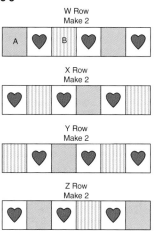

Figure 9

2. Repeat step 1 with one A, two B and three C heart rectangles to make two X rows, again referring to Figure 9.

3. Repeat step 1 with one A, two B and three C heart rectangles to make two Y rows, again referring to Figure 9.

4. Repeat step 1 with two A, one B and three C heart rectangles to make two Z rows, again referring to Figure 9.

5. Join one each W, X, Y and Z rows to complete the top half of the quilt top referring to Figure 10; press seams in one direction. Repeat in the same order to complete the bottom half of the quilt top. Join the two halves to complete the pieced center referring to the Placement Diagram for positioning on halves; press seam in the same direction as other rows.

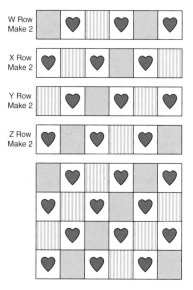

Figure 10

6. Sew a D strip to the top and bottom and E strips to opposite long sides of the pieced center; press seams toward D and E strips.

7. Sew an H strip to each short end of each appliquéd F strip; press seams toward H strips.

8. Sew the F-H strips to opposite long sides of the pieced center; press seams toward E strips.

9. Sew an H strip to each short end of each appliquéd G strip and add a Flower Corner block to the H end as shown in Figure 11; press seams toward H strips.

Figure 11

10. Sew the G-H/block strips to the top and bottom of the pieced center referring to the Placement Diagram for positioning; press seams away from the G-H/block strips.

11. Sew J strips to the top and bottom and K strips to opposite long sides to complete the pieced top; press seams toward J and K strips.

12. Press quilt top on both sides; check for proper seam pressing and trim all loose threads.

13. Sandwich batting between the stitched top and the prepared backing piece; pin or baste layers together to hold. Quilt as desired by hand or machine. *Note: The sample quilt was machine-quilted in the ditch along all seam lines and on leaf vein lines with clear nylon monofilament in the needle and white thread in the bobbin. It was hand-quilted ¼" from each appliqué shape and ¼" from seams inside the appliquéd C rectangles and F and G border strips using dark pink quilting thread.*

14. When quilting is complete, remove pins or basting. Trim batting and backing edges fabric even with raw edges of quilt top.

15. Join binding strips on short ends with diagonal seams to make one long strip; trim seams to ¼" and press seams open.

16. Fold the binding strip in half with wrong sides together along length; press.

17. Sew binding to quilt edges, matching raw edges, mitering corners and overlapping ends.

18. Fold binding to the back side and stitch in place to finish. ▓

Sleepytime Lambs Baby Quilt
Placement Diagram 39" x 50"

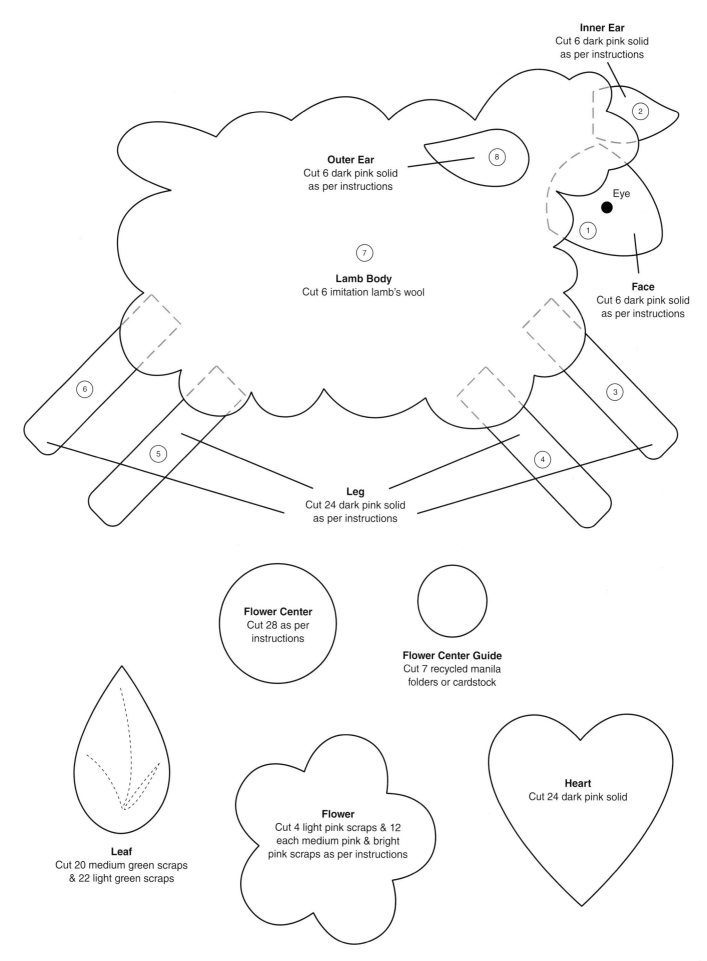

Inner Ear
Cut 6 dark pink solid
as per instructions

Outer Ear
Cut 6 dark pink solid
as per instructions

Eye

Face
Cut 6 dark pink solid
as per instructions

Lamb Body
Cut 6 imitation lamb's wool

Leg
Cut 24 dark pink solid
as per instructions

Flower Center
Cut 28 as per
instructions

Flower Center Guide
Cut 7 recycled manila
folders or cardstock

Leaf
Cut 20 medium green scraps
& 22 light green scraps

Flower
Cut 4 light pink scraps & 12
each medium pink & bright
pink scraps as per instructions

Heart
Cut 24 dark pink solid

Magic Maze

Two simple blocks and strategic color placement yield an interlocking double ring. Time to get out your scraps.

DESIGN BY BEA YURKERWICH

QUILTED BY DIANNA LUKEN

PATTERN SPECIFICATIONS

Skill Level: Beginner
Quilt Size: 60" x 60"
Block Size: 16" x 16"
Number of Blocks: 9

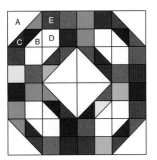

Magic Maze
16" x 16" Block
Make 9

MATERIALS

- 2 yards total assorted scraps (at least 3" in diameter)
- ⅝ yard black solid
- 1¼ yards fuchsia print
- 1⅜ yards cream tonal
- Backing 68" x 68"
- Batting 68" x 68"
- Neutral-color all-purpose thread
- Quilting thread
- Basic sewing tools and supplies

Cutting

1. Cut (108) 2⅞" squares from assorted scraps; subcut each square in half on one diagonal to make 216 C triangles.

2. Cut (216) 2½" squares from assorted scraps.

3. Cut six 2¼" by fabric width strips black solid for binding.

4. Cut six 6½" by fabric width F/G strips from fuchsia print.

5. Cut five 4⅞" by fabric width strips from cream tonal; subcut into (36) 4⅞" squares. Cut each square in half on one diagonal to make 72 A triangles.

6. Cut three 2⅞" by fabric width strips from cream tonal; subcut into (36) 2⅞" squares. Cut each square in half on one diagonal to make 72 B triangles.

7. Cut five 2½" by fabric width strips from cream tonal; subcut into (72) 2½" D squares.

Completing the Blocks

1. Select two each A and B triangles, six C triangles, two D squares and six E squares.

2. Sew B to C along the diagonal; press seam toward C. Repeat to make two B-C units.

3. Sew a C triangle to each C side of each B-C unit to make a B-C triangle unit as shown in Figure 1; press seams away from the B-C square. Repeat to make two B-C triangle units.

Figure 1

4. Sew A to each B-C triangle unit to complete two A units as shown in Figure 2; press seams toward A.

Figure 2

5. Join one D square with three E squares, as shown in Figure 3, to complete one D-E unit; press seams in rows in opposite directions, and then in one direction. Repeat to make two D-E units.

Make 2

Figure 3

6. Join one A unit with a D-E unit to make a row as shown in Figure 4; press seams toward the D-E unit. Repeat to make two rows.

Make 2

Figure 4

7. Join the rows to complete a block quarter as shown in Figure 5; press seam in one direction.

Figure 5

8. Repeat steps 1–7 to complete four block quarters.

9. Join two block quarters to make a row referring to Figure 6; press seam in one direction. Repeat to make two rows; join the rows to complete one Magic Maze block. Press seam in one direction.

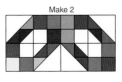

Make 2

Figure 6

10. Repeat steps 1–9 to complete nine Magic Maze blocks.

Completing the Quilt Top

1. Arrange and join three Magic Maze blocks to make a row; press seams in one direction. Repeat to make three rows.

2. Join the rows with seams alternating directions to complete the pieced center; press row seams in one direction.

3. Join the F/G strips on short ends to make one long strip; press seams open. Subcut strip into two 48½" F strips and two 60½" G strips.

4. Sew F strips to opposite sides and G strips to the top and bottom of the pieced center; press seams toward F and G strips to complete the pieced top.

Completing the Quilt

1. Press quilt top on both sides; check for proper seam pressing and trim all loose threads.

2. Sandwich batting between the stitched top and the prepared backing piece; pin or baste layers together to hold. Quilt on marked lines and as desired by hand or machine.

3. When quilting is complete, remove pins or basting. Trim batting and backing fabric edges even with raw edges of quilt top.

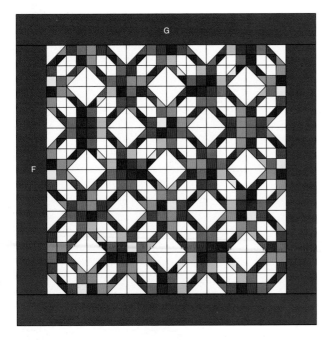

Magic Maze
Placement Diagram 60" x 60"

4. Join binding strips on short ends with diagonal seams to make one long strip; trim seams to ¼" and press seams open.

5. Fold the binding strip in half with wrong sides together along length; press.

6. Sew binding to quilt edges, matching raw edges, mitering corners and overlapping ends.

7. Fold binding to the back side and stitch in place to finish. ■

Friendship Stars Backpack

Backpacks are great totes. Who says they can't be attractive accessories as well?

DESIGN BY KATE LAUCOMER

PROJECT SPECIFICATIONS

Skill Level: Intermediate
Backpack Size: Approximately 12" x 15"
Block Size: 3" x 3"
Number of Blocks: 3

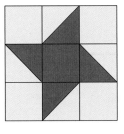

Star
3" x 3" Block
Make 3

MATERIALS

- 1 fat quarter tan check for block piecing
- ⅓ yard contrasting black plaid for flap and block piecing
- ⅝ yard black-and-tan plaid for backpack body
- All-purpose thread to match fabrics
- 32" (or 64" if 2 straps are desired) black strapping or webbing
- 9" black zipper
- 1 (1") black button
- 1 hook-and-loop dot (optional)
- 3½" x 12" rectangle needlepoint plastic
- Basic sewing tools and supplies

Cutting

1. Cut one 1½" x 21" strip tan check; subcut strip into (12) 1½" A squares tan check.

2. Cut one 2½" x 21" strip tan check; subcut strip into six 2½" B squares.

3. Cut one 2½" by fabric width strip contrasting black plaid; subcut strip into six 2½" D squares and six 1½" x 1½" C squares.

4. Cut a 3½" x 9½" E strip tan check.

5. Cut one 15½" x 30½" F strip black-and-tan plaid.

6. Cut one 4½" by fabric width strip contrasting black plaid; subcut strip into two 7½" G strips.

7. Prepare a template for the backpack bottom and cut as directed on pattern.

Completing the Blocks

1. Draw a diagonal line from corner to corner on the wrong side of each B square.

2. Place a B square right sides together with a D square and stitch ¼" on each side of the marked line as shown in Figure 1; cut apart on the marked line and press open with seam toward D to make two B-D units, again referring to Figure 1.

Figure 1

3. Trim the two B-D units to 1½" x 1½" square as shown in Figure 2.

Figure 2

4. Repeat steps 2 and 3 to complete a total of 12 B-D units.

5. Select, arrange and join one C square, four A squares and four B-D units in rows referring to Figure 3; press seams toward A and C squares. Join the rows to complete one Star block; press seams in one direction.

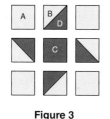

Figure 3

6. Repeat step 5 to complete a total of three Star blocks.

Completing the Backpack

1. Join the three Star blocks to make the block strip as shown in Figure 4; press seams to one side.

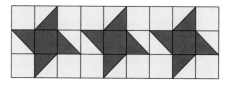

Figure 4

2. Place the E strip right sides together with the block strip. Stitch around edges, leaving a 3" opening on one side; clip corners. Turn right side out through the opening; press flat. Hand-stitch opening closed to finish the block strip.

3. Pin the block strip on the F strip 2¼" from the edge on one 30½" edge and 3½" from the 15½" edge as shown in Figure 5.

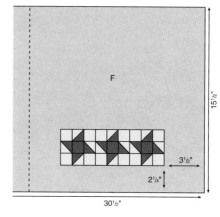

Figure 5

4. Stitch around three sides of the block strip, leaving the top edge open for a shallow pocket, or leave open on one end for glasses or cellphone referring to Figure 6. Sew a hook-and-loop dot at the opening, if desired.

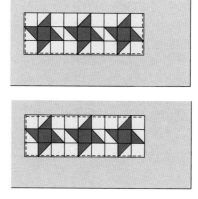

Figure 6

5. Bring the right sides of the short ends of F together and sew 2½" up from the bottom and 4" down from the top as shown in Figure 7; press seam allowances open.

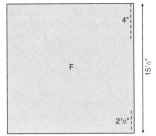

Figure 7

6. Insert zipper for backpack side opening in the seam opening referring to the instructions with the zipper.

7. With the zipper at one side, find the top center front and back and mark each with a pin as shown in Figure 8; measure out each direction, front and back, 3½" from the center pins and mark with pins, again referring to Figure 8.

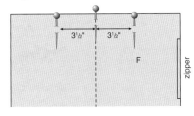

Figure 8

8. Pleat each side in to meet the pins, front and back, as shown in Figure 9; sew in place ½" from the top edge, again referring to Figure 9.

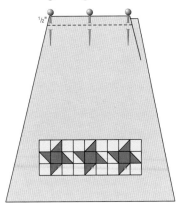

Figure 9

9. Fold all seams over to the back ½"; zigzag over raw edges.

10. Measure and mark 1¼" up on each 4½" end and 3¾" to the center of the 7½" side of each of the G rectangles as shown in Figure 10.

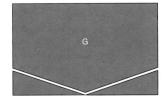

Figure 10

11. Cut on marked lines to make the two flap pieces as shown in Figure 11.

Figure 11

12. Place the flap pieces right sides together and stitch all around, leaving a 3" opening on the top 7½" edge as shown in Figure 12; clip corners.

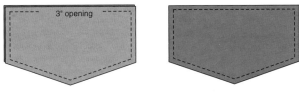

Figure 12   **Figure 13**

13. Turn the flap unit right side out through the opening; press flat. Turn opening to the inside and hand-stitch closed. Topstitch flap piece ¼" from all edges as shown in Figure 13.

14. Position flap on the front of the backpack, extending the top edge ¾" over onto the back; pin in place.

15. Center strap (or straps) under the flap on the back side of the backpack. Remove pins and flap and stitch strips securely to the top of the backpack.

16. Re-pin the flap in place and stitch in place on the back side. Fold the flap over to the backpack front and pin in place.

17. Sew button at center point of the center front of the flap through all layers. ***Note:*** *The top of the* *backpack is not left open. The zipper opening is used to insert things into the backpack.*

18. Fold one of the backpack bottom pieces to find the centers and mark with pins as shown in Figure 14.

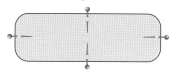

Figure 14

19. Pin the bottom edges of the strap (straps) in place at the lower edge of the backpack. Open the zipper of the backpack and turn wrong side out through the zipper opening. Find sides, center front and center back of backpack and mark with pins as in step 18.

20. Match the pins of the backpack with pins of backpack bottom and pin layers with right sides together all around.

21. Sew carefully around the bottom, reinforcing seams over the straps. Turn right side out through zipper opening.

22. Place the needlepoint plastic rectangle between the two remaining fabric pieces with wrong sides facing the needlepoint plastic. Sew around edge of plastic without sewing on the plastic; trim seam to ⅛".

23. Satin-stitch over raw edges of the stitched unit and place inside the bottom of the backpack; hand-stitch in place to secure and complete the backpack. ▨

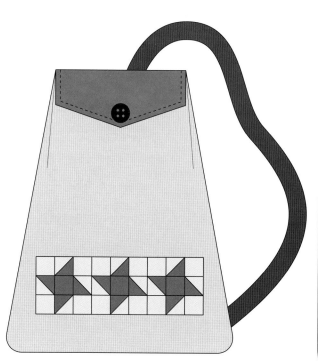

Friendship Stars Backpack
Placement Diagram
Approximately 12" x 15"

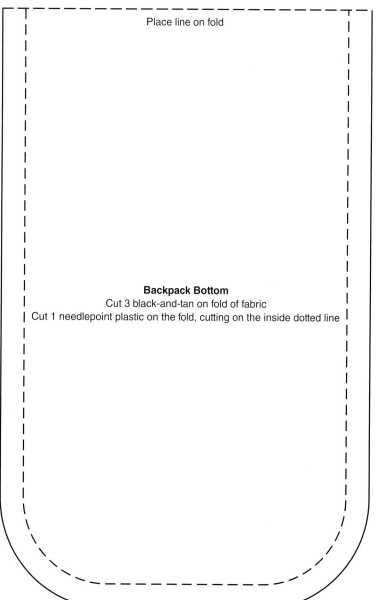

Place line on fold

Backpack Bottom
Cut 3 black-and-tan on fold of fabric
Cut 1 needlepoint plastic on the fold, cutting on the inside dotted line

Diamond Candy

Tutti-frutti, lemon lime, cherry and tangerine are such pretty colors—just like penny candy.

DESIGN BY CINDI RANG

PROJECT SPECIFICATIONS

Skill Level: Intermediate
Quilt Size: 68" x 88"
Block Size: 10" x 10"
Number of Blocks: 48

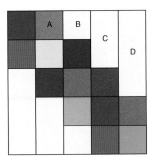

Diamond Candy
10" x 10" Block
Make 48

MATERIALS

- ⅓ yard each 18 different bright-color batiks
- 4 yards pale yellow batik
- Backing 74" x 94"
- Batting 74" x 94"
- Neutral-color all-purpose thread
- Quilting thread
- Basic sewing tools and supplies

Cutting

1. From each different bright-color batik, cut three 2½" by fabric width strips; subcut into (41) 2½" A squares each fabric color.

2. Cut six 2½" by fabric width strips from pale yellow; subcut into (96) 2½" B squares.

3. Cut six 4½" by fabric width strips from pale yellow; subcut into (96) 2½" x 4½" C rectangles.

4. Cut six 6½" by fabric width strips from pale yellow; subcut into (96) 2½" x 6½" D rectangles.

5. Cut one 16½" by fabric width rectangle from pale yellow; subcut into (14) 2½" x 16½" E strips.

6. Cut eight 2½" by fabric width F/G strips.

Special Instructions

1. Select 68 A squares in a variety of colors; mark a diagonal line from corner to corner on the wrong side of each square. Set aside these marked squares for later use.

Piecing the Blocks

1. To make one Diamond Candy block, select 13 A squares in a variety of colors. Join two A squares to make a 2A unit; press seam in one direction. Repeat to make two 2A units.

2. Join three A squares to make a 3A unit; press seams in one direction. Repeat to make three 3A units.

3. Sew a 2A unit to one end of two D rectangles; press seams toward the 2A units.

4. Sew a 3A unit to one end of two C rectangles; press seams toward the 3A units.

5. Sew a B square to each end of one 3A unit; press seams toward the 3A unit.

6. Arrange and join the pieced units in rows to complete one Diamond Candy block as shown in Figure 1; press seams in one direction.

Figure 1

7. Repeat steps 1–6 to complete 48 Diamond Candy blocks.

Completing the Quilt Top

1. Select four Diamond Candy blocks and set aside for corners.

2. Select 20 Diamond Candy blocks.

3. Place a marked A square on one D corner of one block as shown in Figure 2; stitch on the marked line, again referring to Figure 2.

Figure 2

4. Trim seam allowance to ¼" and press A to the right side as shown in Figure 3. Repeat on 20 blocks.

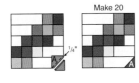

Make 20

Figure 3

Diamond Candy
Placement Diagram 68" x 88"

5. Repeat steps 3 and 4 with A on each D corner of the remaining 24 blocks referring to Figure 4.

Figure 4

6. Arrange and join the blocks in eight rows of six blocks each, placing blocks with triangles in rows referring to Figure 5; press seams in adjacent rows in opposite directions.

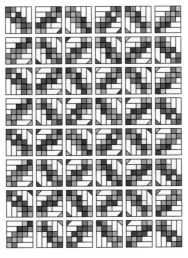

Figure 5

7. Join the rows to complete the pieced center; press seams in one direction.

8. Sew an A square to each end of an E strip; press seams toward A; repeat for all E strips.

9. Join four A-E units on short ends to make one long A-E border strip as shown in Figure 6; press seams in one direction. Repeat to make two long A-E strips.

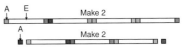

Figure 6

10. Sew a long A-E strip to opposite sides of the pieced center; press seams toward the long A-E strips.

11. Repeat step 9 with three A-E units to make two short A-E strips, adding an A square to each end of the strips, again referring to Figure 6.

12. Sew a short A-E strip to the top and bottom of the pieced center; press seams toward short A-E strips.

13. Join the F/G strips on short ends to make one long strip; press seams open. Subcut strip into two 84½" F strips and two 68½" G strips.

14. Sew an F strip to opposite long sides and G strips to the top and bottom of the pieced center to complete the pieced top.

Completing the Quilt

1. Press quilt top on both sides; check for proper seam pressing and trim all loose threads.

2. Sandwich batting between the stitched top and the prepared backing piece; pin or baste layers together to hold. Mark quilting design and quilt as desired by hand or machine.

3. When quilting is complete, remove pins or basting. Trim batting and backing fabric edges even with raw edges of quilt top.

4. Join binding strips on short ends with diagonal seams to make one long strip; trim seams to ¼" and press seams open.

5. Fold the binding strip in half with wrong sides together along length; press.

6. Sew binding to quilt edges, matching raw edges, mitering corners and overlapping ends.

7. Fold binding to the back side and stitch in place to finish. ■

Take Your Time

Enjoy your quilting time with these special Take Your Time projects. Soothe those frazzled nerves with Puppy Dog Tails, 3-D Tumbling Blocks or Windflowers. These 5 lovely projects will allow you to work at your own speed and still see progress as you use your favorite stash and scraps of fabric to complete fabulous gifts.

Puppy Dog Tails

Little boys will love this quilt full of puppies and snails. Change all the blue fabrics to pink and little girls will be equally charmed by this delightful nursery-rhyme quilt.

DESIGN BY BARBARA CLAYTON

PROJECT SPECIFICATIONS

Skill Level: Advanced
Quilt Size: 43" x 43"
Block Size: 9" x 9"
Number of Blocks: 9

MATERIALS

- Scraps yellow print and light blue print
- 1 fat quarter dark blue mottled
- ¼ yard light blue with white dots
- ¼ yard dark blue print
- ¼ yard medium green print
- ⅓ yard medium blue print 1
- ⅓ yard medium blue print 2
- ⅜ yard light green print
- ½ yard white with light blue dots
- ½ yard solid white
- ½ yard solid medium green
- 1 yard baby blue with dots
- Backing 51" x 51"
- Batting 51" x 51"
- All-purpose thread to match fabrics
- Royal blue quilting thread
- 2 skeins royal blue hand-embroidery floss
- ¼" press bar
- Basic sewing tools and supplies

Cutting

1. Cut two 3" by fabric width strips light blue with white dots; subcut strips into four 7" C rectangles and four 9½" B rectangles.

2. Cut one 3½" by fabric width strip dark blue print; subcut strip into four 3½" G squares. Trim remainder of strip to 3¼" wide and cut four 3¼" K squares. Save scraps for appliqué.

Puppy Dog
9" x 9"
Make 2 and 2 reversed

Snake
9" x 9"
Make 1

Reverse Snail
9" x 9"
Make 2

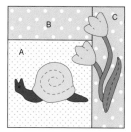

Snail
9" x 9"
Make 2 and 2 reversed

3. Cut one 3¼" by fabric width strip medium green print; subcut strip into eight 3¼" L squares. Trim remainder of strip to 2¾" wide and cut one 2¾" x 9½" E rectangle. Save scraps for appliqué.

4. Cut two 3½" by fabric width strips medium blue print 1; subcut strips into (20) 3½" P squares.

5. Cut two 3⅝" by fabric width strips medium blue print 1; subcut strips into (20) 3⅝" I squares. Save scraps for appliqué.

6. Cut two 3½" by fabric width strips medium blue print 2; subcut strips into (20) 3½" Q squares. Save scraps for appliqué.

7. Cut one 9½" by fabric width strip light green print; subcut strip into four 9½" F squares.

8. Cut six 5"- and five 3"-long, 1"-wide bias strips from solid medium green for appliqué flower stems. Save remainder of fabric for appliqué.

9. Cut one 7" by fabric width strip from white with light blue dots; subcut into four 7" A squares. Trim remainder to 6¾" wide and cut one 6¾" x 9½" D rectangle.

10. Cut two 3⅝" by fabric width strips white with light blue dots; subcut strips into (20) 3⅝" J squares.

11. Cut one 9½" by fabric width strip baby blue with dots; subcut strip into (12) 9½" H rectangles.

12. Cut four 1½" by fabric width strips baby blue with dots. Trim strips to make two 1½" x 41" M strips and two 1½" x 39" N strips.

13. Cut four 3½" by fabric width strips baby blue with dots. Subcut strips into (40) 3½" O squares.

Completing the Appliqué Blocks

1. Stitch C to top of A and press seam toward C. Repeat to make four A-C units.

2. Stitch B to the right edge of an A-C unit, as shown in Figure 1, to make a snail background; press seam toward B. Repeat to make a second snail background.

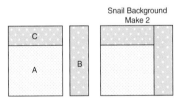

Snail Background
Make 2

Figure 1

3. Stitch B to left edge of an A-C unit, as shown in Figure 2, to make a reversed snail background; press seam toward B. Repeat to make a second reversed snail background.

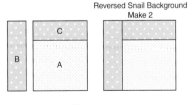

Reversed Snail Background
Make 2

Figure 2

4. Stitch E to the bottom of D and press seam toward E to make one snake background referring to the Snake block diagram.

5. Set all backgrounds aside.

6. Using your favorite appliqué method, prepare appliqué shapes referring to appliqué motifs on pages 151–153 for cutting instructions. **Note:** *Appliqué motifs have been reversed for fusible appliqué. Seam allowances should be added to individual pieces for turned appliqué.*

7. Apply Puppy Dog appliqué to the center of each G square using chosen appliqué technique and referring to appliqué motif for positioning.

8. Apply Snail appliqué to the center of the A square in the snail backgrounds and reversed snail backgrounds. **Note:** *Snails should face away from the B rectangle in the blocks.*

9. Fold each appliqué flower stem in half wrong sides together along length and stitch. Insert ¼" pressing bar into stem and press with seam flat and centered on one side. Apply stems, leaves and flowers to B rectangle area of snail blocks referring to block and Placement Diagram.

10. Refer to block diagram and apply snake and two flower appliqués to the snake background.

11. Hand-embroider the puppy dog, snake and snail eyes as marked on patterns with two strands royal blue embroidery floss and a satin stitch to complete each appliquéd block.

Completing the Pieced Border

1. Draw a diagonal line on wrong side of each J square. Stitch J and I squares wrong sides together ¼" on either side of the marked line on J. Cut on the marked line to make two I-J squares. Press seams toward I. Repeat to make 40 I-J units referring to Figure 3.

I-J units
Make 40

Figure 3

2. Join five I-J units, with I in the bottom right corner, to make a right-side I-J strip referring to Figure 4. Repeat to make four right-side strips.

Right-side I-J Strip
Make 4

Figure 4

3. Join five I-J units, with I in the bottom left corner, to make a left-side I-J strip referring to Figure 5. Repeat to make four left-side strips.

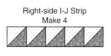

Left-side I-J strip
Make 4

Figure 5

4. Join one each right- and left-side I-J strip with right sides together, matching the J triangles to make a side strip as shown in Figure 6.

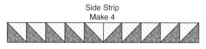

Side Strip
Make 4

Figure 6

5. Stitch an L square to both ends of two side strips to make top and bottom borders. Stitch first an L square and then a K square to each end of the remaining two side strips to make side borders.

Completing the Quilt Top

1. Join one each Reversed Snail block, Snail block and Dog block and two H rectangles to make the top row as shown in Figure 7. Press seams toward H. Repeat to make the bottom row.

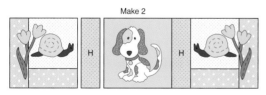

Make 2

Figure 7

2. Join two each Dog blocks and H rectangles and the Snake block to make the center row referring to Figure 8; press seams toward H .

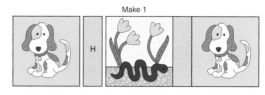

Make 1

Figure 8

3. Join three H rectangles and two G squares to make a sashing row as shown in Figure 9; repeat to make a second sashing row Press seams toward H.

Make 2

Figure 9

4. Join rows referring to the Placement Diagram for positioning of rows; press seams toward the sashing rows to complete the quilt center.

5. Stitch top and bottom pieced borders to the quilt center; press seams toward quilt center.

6. Stitch side strips to opposite sides of the quilt center; press seams toward quilt center.

7. Stitch N strips to opposite sides of the quilt center; press seams toward N. Stitch M strips to the top and bottom of the quilt center; press seams toward M.

8. Mark chosen quilting pattern on the completed top.

Completing the Quilt

1. Fold each O, P and Q square in half diagonally twice referring to Figure 10 to make 80 Prairie Points.

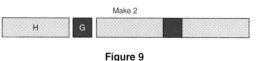

Figure 10

2. Beginning in a corner with an O Prairie Point and alternating with P and Q points, arrange and pin 20 Prairie Points to one side of the quilt top, matching raw edges to quilt edges and referring to Figure 11 and the Placement Diagram. Overlap the points evenly to fit. Baste to hold. Repeat on all four sides of the quilt top.

Figure 11

3. Center the quilt backing wrong side down on the batting. Center the quilt top right sides together with the backing and pin layers together around quilt top edges to hold.

4. Stitch around quilt top edges, leaving a 10" opening on one side. Trim backing and batting even with quilt top edges. Trim corners and batting close to stitching. Turn quilt layers right side out through opening, pulling Prairie Points away from the quilt top.

5. Turn opening seam allowances to inside of quilt and press all edges flat. Hand-stitch opening closed.

6. Pin or baste layers together to hold. Quilt on marked lines and as desired by hand or machine. When quilting is complete, remove pins or basting to finish. ■

Puppy Tails Baby Quilt
Placement Diagram 43" x 43"

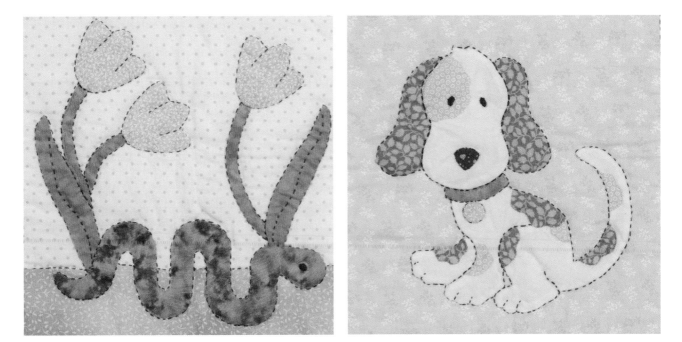

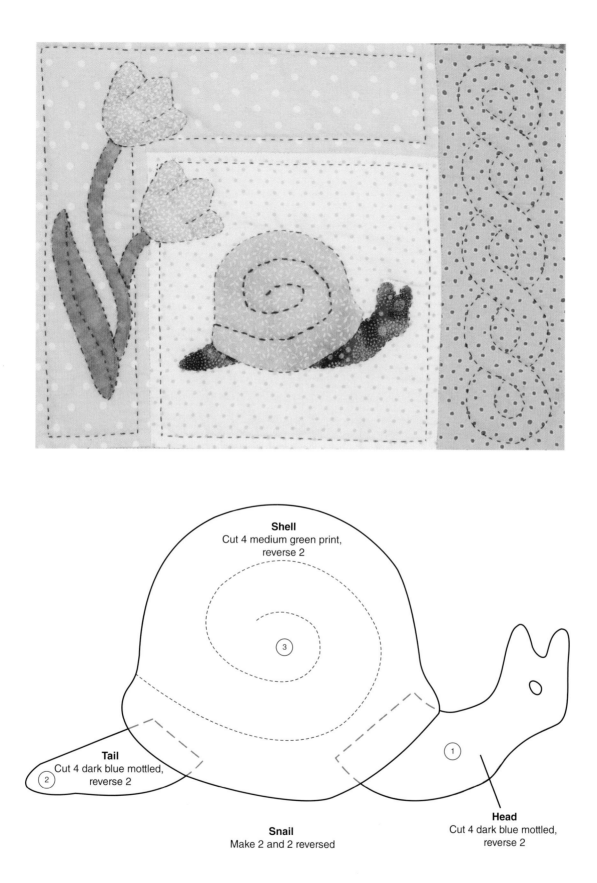

Shell
Cut 4 medium green print,
reverse 2

Tail
Cut 4 dark blue mottled,
reverse 2

Head
Cut 4 dark blue mottled,
reverse 2

Snail
Make 2 and 2 reversed

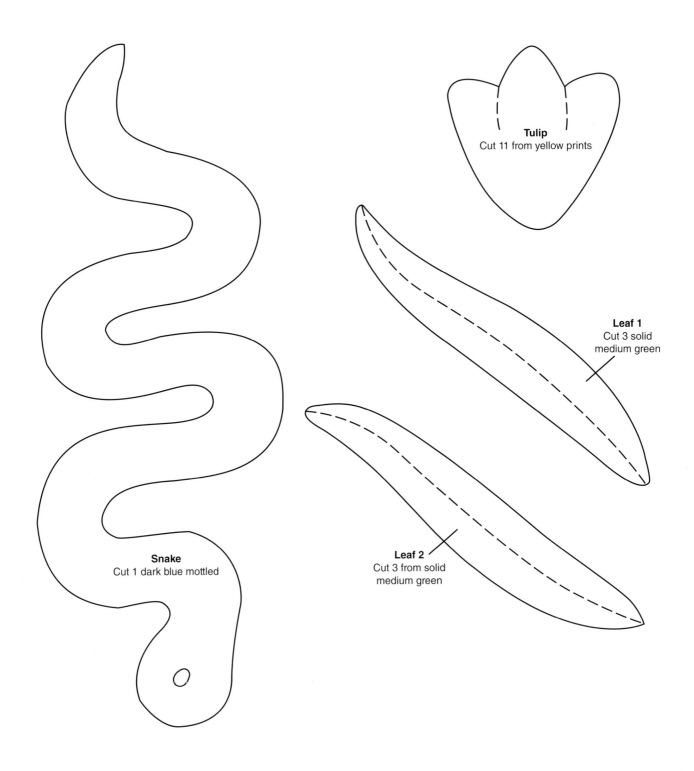

Tulip
Cut 11 from yellow prints

Leaf 1
Cut 3 solid
medium green

Leaf 2
Cut 3 from solid
medium green

Snake
Cut 1 dark blue mottled

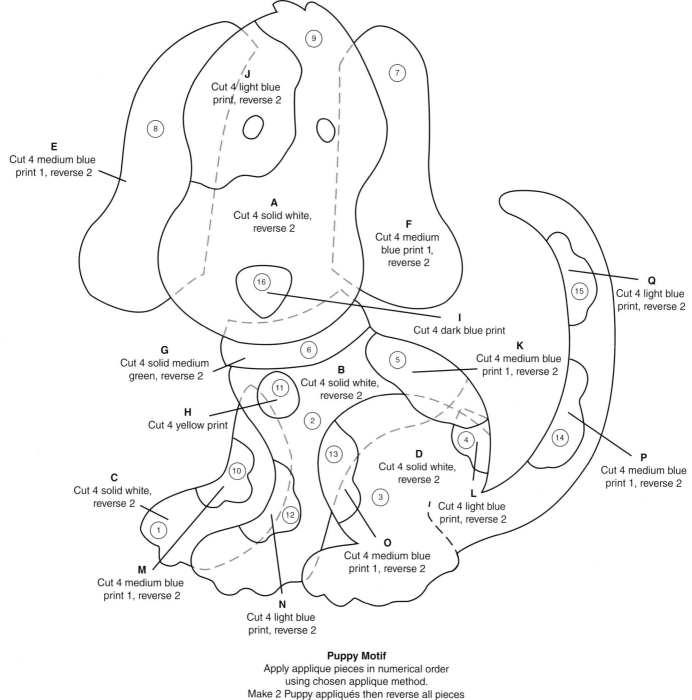

E
Cut 4 medium blue
print 1, reverse 2

J
Cut 4 light blue
print, reverse 2

A
Cut 4 solid white,
reverse 2

F
Cut 4 medium
blue print 1,
reverse 2

Q
Cut 4 light blue
print, reverse 2

I
Cut 4 dark blue print

G
Cut 4 solid medium
green, reverse 2

B
Cut 4 solid white,
reverse 2

K
Cut 4 medium blue
print 1, reverse 2

H
Cut 4 yellow print

C
Cut 4 solid white,
reverse 2

D
Cut 4 solid white,
reverse 2

L
Cut 4 light blue
print, reverse 2

P
Cut 4 medium blue
print 1, reverse 2

M
Cut 4 medium blue
print 1, reverse 2

O
Cut 4 medium blue
print 1, reverse 2

N
Cut 4 light blue
print, reverse 2

Puppy Motif
Apply applique pieces in numerical order
using chosen applique method.
Make 2 Puppy appliqués then reverse all pieces
to make two Reverse Puppy appliqué blocks.

Windflowers

Grandma would be happy to see that fabric companies are reproducing fabrics similar to the ones she used in the early part of the 1900s.

DESIGN BY JULIE WEAVER

QUILTED BY MARIE BREWER, PINE NEEDLE QUILTING

PROJECT SPECIFICATIONS

Skill Level: Intermediate
Quilt Size: 80" x 96"
Block Sizes: 10" x 10" and 8" x 8"
Number of Blocks: 4 and 41

MATERIALS

- 1 fat quarter each 5 red prints
- 1 fat quarter each 8 pink prints
- 1 fat quarter each 4 blue prints
- 1 fat quarter each 12 lavender prints
- 1 fat quarter each 12 yellow prints
- 1⅛ yards green print
- 1⅓ yards blue print
- 2¼ yards cream-with-pink dot
- 2⅓ yards cream tonal
- Backing 86" x 102"
- Batting 86" x 102"
- Neutral-color all-purpose thread
- Quilting thread
- Basic sewing tools and supplies

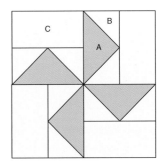

Corner Pinwheel
10" x 10" Block
Make 4

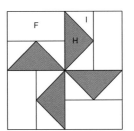

Pinwheel
8" x 8" Block
Make 1 red & 8 pink

Bordered Pinwheel
8" x 8" Block
Make 4 blue, 4 red,
12 yellow & 12 lavender

Cutting

1. Cut four 2½" x 4½" H rectangles from one of the five red prints.

2. Cut two 2⅞" E squares from each of the remaining four red prints.

3. Cut 21 total 2½" x 10½" M rectangles from the five red prints.

4. Cut four 2½" x 4½" H rectangles from each of eight pink prints.

5. Cut 28 total 2½" x 10½" M rectangles from the eight pink prints.

6. Cut two 2⅞" E squares from each of four blue prints.

7. Cut 13 total 2½" x 10½" M rectangles from the four blue prints.

8. Cut two 2⅞" E squares from each of 12 lavender prints.

9. Cut 34 total 2½" x 10½" M rectangles from the 12 lavender prints.

10. Cut two 2⅞" E squares from each of 12 yellow prints.

11. Cut 33 total 2½" x 10½" M rectangles from the 12 yellow prints.

12. Cut three 3" by fabric width strips from green print; subcut into (16) 3" x 5½" A rectangles.

13. Cut eight 2½" by fabric width G strips from the green print.

14. Cut two 2½" by fabric width strips from green print. Subcut the strips into seven 2½" x 10½" M rectangles.

15. Cut seven 2½" by fabric width K/L strips and nine 2¼" by fabric width strips for binding from blue print.

16. Cut six 8½" by fabric width strips from cream-with-pink dot; subcut strips into (22) 8½" J squares.

17. Cut three 3" by fabric width strips from cream-with-pink dot; subcut strips into (32) 3" B squares.

18. Cut three 5½" by fabric width strips from cream-with-pink dot; subcut strips into (16) 3" x 5½" C rectangles.

19. Cut five 2½" by fabric width strips from cream tonal; subcut strips into (72) 2½" I squares.

20. Cut four 4½" by fabric width F strips and seven 4½" by fabric width strips from cream tonal. Subcut the seven strips into (100) 2½" x 4½" F rectangles.

21. Cut five 2⅞" by fabric width strips from cream tonal; subcut into (64) 2⅞" D squares.

Completing the Corner Pinwheel Blocks

1. Mark a diagonal line on the wrong side of all B, D and I squares; set aside D and I squares for Bordered Pinwheel and Pinwheel blocks.

2. Referring to Figure 1, place B right sides together on one end of A; stitch on the marked line. Trim seam allowance to ¼"; press B to the right side.

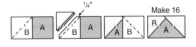

Figure 1

3. Repeat step 2 on the remaining end of A to complete an A-B unit, again referring to Figure 1. Repeat to make 16 A-B units.

4. Sew C to an A-B unit as shown in Figure 2; press seam toward C. Repeat to make 16-A-B-C units.

Figure 2

5. To complete one Corner Pinwheel block, join two A-B-C units to make a row as shown in Figure 3; press seams in one direction. Repeat to make two rows.

Figure 3

6. Join the rows referring to the block drawing to complete one Corner Pinwheel block; repeat to make four blocks.

Completing the Pinwheel Blocks

1. Using H for A, I for B and F for C, complete one red and eight pink Pinwheel blocks referring to the instructions for Completing the Corner Pinwheel Blocks and Figure 4.

Figure 4

Completing the Bordered Pinwheel Blocks

1. Place a D square right sides together on an E square; stitch ¼" on each side of the marked line on D as shown in Figure 5.

Figure 5

2. Cut apart on the marked line and press units open with seams toward E to make two D-E units, again referring to Figure 5. Repeat with remaining D and E pieces to make 128 D-E units.

3. Sew an F strip between two G strips with right sides together along the length; press seams toward G. Repeat to make four strip sets.

4. Subcut the F-G strip sets into (64) 2½" F-G units as shown in Figure 6.

Figure 6

5. To complete one Bordered Pinwheel block, join two matching D-E units as shown in Figure 7; press seam in one direction. Repeat; join the units, again referring to Figure 7, to complete the center unit. Press seam to one side.

Figure 7

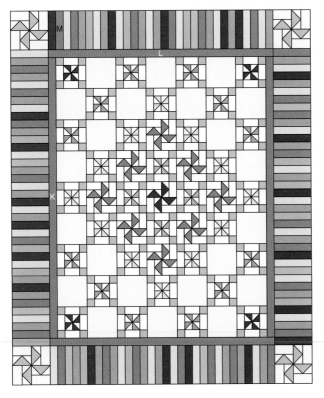

Windflowers
Placement Diagram 80" x 96"

6. Sew F to opposite sides of the center unit to complete the center row as shown in Figure 8; press seams toward F.

Figure 8

7. Sew an F-G unit to opposite sides of the center row to complete one Bordered Pinwheel block; press seams toward F-G units. Repeat to make four each blue and red and 12 each yellow and lavender blocks.

Completing the Quilt

1. Arrange and join the blocks and J squares in nine rows referring to Figure 9 and the Placement Diagram, being careful of color positioning of blocks; press seams toward J.

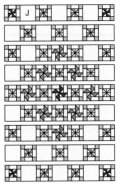

Figure 9

2. Join the rows referring to the Placement Diagram to complete the pieced center; press seams in one direction.

3. Join the K/L strips on short ends to make one long strip; press seams open. Subcut strip into two 72½" K strips and two 60½" L strips.

4. Sew K to opposite sides and L to the top and bottom of the pieced center; press seams toward K and L strips.

5. Join 38 M pieces to make an M side strip; press seams in one direction. Repeat to make two M side strips.

6. Sew an M side strip to opposite long sides of the pieced center; press seams toward the M side strips.

7. Join 30 M pieces to make a top strip; press seams in one direction.

8. Sew a Corner Pinwheel block to each end of the M top strip; press seams toward the M top strip. Repeat to make an M bottom strip.

9. Sew the M top strip to the top and the M bottom strip to the bottom of the pieced center to complete the pieced top; press seams toward the M strips.

10. Press quilt top on both sides; check for proper seam pressing and trim all loose threads.

11. Sandwich batting between the stitched top and the prepared backing piece; pin or baste layers together to hold. Quilt on marked lines and as desired by hand or machine.

12. When quilting is complete, remove pins or basting. Trim batting and backing fabric edges even with raw edges of quilt top.

13. Join binding strips on short ends with diagonal seams to make one long strip; trim seams to ¼" and press seams open.

14. Fold the binding strip in half with wrong sides together along length; press.

15. Sew binding to quilt edges, matching raw edges, mitering corners and overlapping ends.

16. Fold binding to the back side and stitch in place to finish. ■

Skins & Stones Throw

This throw is destined to be a favorite. It has a masculine feel that any man can relate to.

DESIGN BY SUE HARVEY & SANDY BOOBAR
MACHINE-QUILTED BY SANDY'S HIDEAWAY QUILTS

PROJECT SPECIFICATIONS

Skill Level: Intermediate
Quilt Size: 71" x 71"
Block Size: 12" x 12"
Number of Blocks: 13

MATERIALS

- ⅜ yard basket-weave print
- ⅝ yard light green mottled
- ⅝ yard tiger stripe
- ⅔ yard leopard print
- 1 yard zebra stripe
- 1⅛ yards gold mottled
- 1¼ yards cream mottled
- 2 yards green/brown mottled
- Batting 79" x 79"
- Backing 79" x 79"
- Neutral-color all-purpose thread
- Quilting thread
- Basic sewing tools and supplies

Cutting

1. Cut one 9" by fabric width strip basket-weave print; subcut strip into three 9" B squares.

2. Cut three 3½" by fabric width strips light green mottled; subcut strips into (36) 3½" E squares.

3. Cut two 3" by fabric width G strips light green mottled.

4. Cut eight 2¼" by fabric width strips tiger stripe for binding.

5. Cut two 9" by fabric width strips leopard print; subcut strips into six 9" A squares.

6. Cut two 6½" by fabric width strips zebra stripe; subcut strips into four 6½" x 12½" C rectangles.

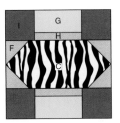

Zebra
12" x 12" Block
Make 4

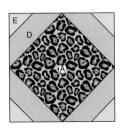

Leopard
12" x 12" Block
Make 6

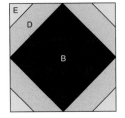

Basket Weave
12" x 12" block
Make 3

7. Cut six 2½" by fabric width P/Q strips zebra stripe.

8. Cut three 6⅞" by fabric width strips gold mottled; subcut strips into (18) 6⅞" squares. Cut each square in half on one diagonal to make 36 D triangles.

9. Cut two 3½" by fabric width strips gold mottled; subcut strips into (16) 3½" F squares.

10. Cut two 1" by fabric width H strips gold mottled.

11. Cut one 19¼" by fabric width strip cream mottled; subcut strip into two 19¼" squares. Cut each square twice diagonally to make eight N triangles.

12. Cut one 10½" by fabric width strip cream mottled; subcut strip into two 10½" squares. Cut each square in half on one diagonal to make four O triangles.

13. Cut six 1½" by fabric width R/S strips cream mottled.

14. Cut two 3½" by fabric width strips green/brown mottled; subcut strips into (16) 3½" I squares.

15. Cut seven 1¼" by fabric width strips green/brown mottled; subcut strips into (18) 1¼" x 12½" J strips and two 1¼" x 14" M strips.

16. Cut two 1¼" x 39½" K strips green/brown mottled.

17. Cut four 1¼" by fabric width L strips green/brown mottled.

18. Cut seven 5½" x 42" T/U strips green/brown mottled.

Completing the Blocks

1. Sew a D triangle to opposite sides of each A square as shown in Figure 1; press seams toward the D triangles. Repeat with D triangles on the remaining sides of A, again referring to Figure 1. Repeat to make six A/D units.

2. Repeat step 1 with B and D to make three B/D units, again referring to Figure 1.

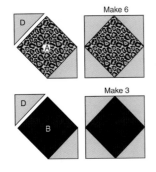

Figure 1

3. Mark a diagonal line from corner to corner on the wrong side of each E and F square.

4. Place a marked E square on a corner of an A/D unit as shown in Figure 2; stitch on the marked lines, trim seam allowances to ¼" and press the E corner to the right side. Repeat on all four corners of the A/D unit to make one Leopard block.

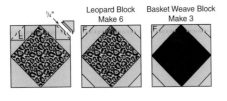

Figure 2

5. Repeat step 4 to make six Leopard blocks, again referring to Figure 2.

6. Repeat step 4 with the B/D units and remaining E pieces to make three Basket Weave blocks, again referring to Figure 2.

7. Place a marked F square on a corner of a C rectangle as shown in Figure 3; stitch on the marked line, trim seam allowance to ¼" and press the F corner to the right side. Repeat on the remaining corners of C to complete a C-F unit. Repeat to make four C-F units.

Figure 3

8. Sew an H strip to a G strip along the length; press seam toward the H strip. Repeat to make a second G-H strip set.

9. Subcut the G-H strip sets into eight 6½" G-H segments as shown in Figure 4.

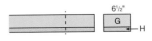

Figure 4

10. Sew an I square to each end of a G-H segment as shown in Figure 5; press seams toward the I squares. Repeat to make 8 G-H-I units.

Figure 5

11. Sew a G-H-I unit to the long sides of each C-F unit to complete four Zebra blocks as shown in Figure 6; press seams toward the G-H-I strips.

Figure 6

Completing the Pieced Center

1. Sew a J strip to opposite sides of each Leopard and Basket Weave block as shown in Figure 7; press seams toward the J strips.

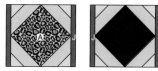

Figure 7

2. Sew an M strip to one edge of two Leopard blocks as shown in Figure 8 to make two Leopard/J/M units; press seams toward M.

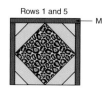

Figure 8

3. Sew an N triangle to each J side of the two Leopard/J/M units as shown in Figure 9; press seams toward the N triangles.

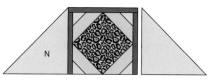

Figure 9

4. Sew an O triangle to the M edge of the Leopard/J/M units as shown in Figure 10 to make two corner units. Press seams toward O triangles.

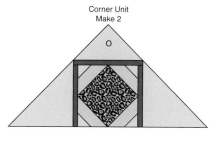

Figure 10

5. Sew a Zebra block between a Leopard and Basket Weave block as shown in Figure 11 to make an X row. Press seams toward Leopard and Basket Weave blocks. Repeat to make a second X row.

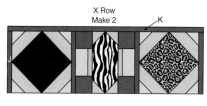

Figure 11

6. Sew a K strip to one long edge of each X row, again referring to Figure 11; press seams toward K strips.

7. Sew an N triangle to both ends of each X row as shown in Figure 12; press seams toward the N triangles.

Figure 12

8. Join the L strips on the short ends to make a long strip; subcut the strip into two 65" L strips.

9. Join two Zebra blocks, two Leopard blocks and one Basket Weave block to make a Y row as shown in Figure 13. Press seams toward J strips. Sew an L strip to both long edges; press seams toward L strips.

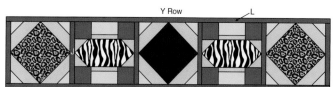

Figure 13

10. Sew an O triangle to both ends of the Y row referring to Figure 14; press seams toward the O triangles.

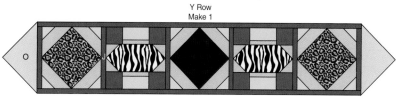

Figure 14

11. Join X and Y rows and corner units as shown in Figure 15 to complete the pieced center; press seams toward X and Y rows.

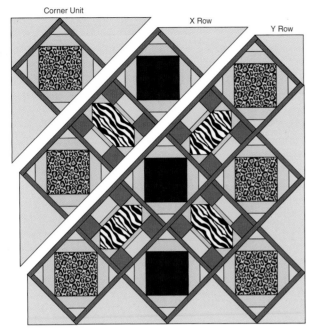

Figure 15

Skins & Stones Throw
Placement Diagram 71" x 71"

Completing the Quilt Top

1. Join the P/Q strips on the short ends to make a long strip; subcut the strip into two 55½" P strips and two 59½" Q strips.

2. Repeat step 1 with the R/S strips to cut two 59½" R strips and two 61½" S strips.

3. Repeat step 1 with the T/U strips to cut two 61½" T strips and two 71½" U strips.

4. Sew the P strips to opposite sides of the pieced center and the Q strips to top and bottom; press seams toward the strips.

5. Repeat to add the R, S, T and U strips in alphabetical order referring to the Placement Diagram, pressing seams toward strips as added to complete the quilt top.

Completing the Quilt

1. Press quilt top on both sides; check for proper seam pressing and trim all loose threads.

2. Sandwich batting between the stitched top and the prepared backing piece; pin or baste layers together to hold. Quilt on marked lines and as desired by hand or machine.

3. When quilting is complete, remove pins or basting. Trim batting and backing fabric edges even with raw edges of quilt top.

4. Join binding strips on short ends with diagonal seams to make one long strip; trim seams to ¼" and press seams open.

5. Fold the binding strip in half with wrong sides together along length; press.

6. Sew binding to quilt edges, matching raw edges, mitering corners and overlapping ends.

7. Fold binding to the back side and stitch in place to finish. ■

Skins & Sticks Pillow

Accent a den with this pillow. You can change out the colors to match any decor.

DESIGN BY SUE HARVEY & SANDY BOOBAR

PROJECT SPECIFICATIONS

Skill Level: Beginner
Pillow Size: 20" x 20"

MATERIALS

- 12 (2½" x 42") coordinating strips
- ¾ yard black solid
- Batting scraps at least 1" x 21"
- Neutral-color all-purpose thread
- 20" pillow form
- Basic sewing tools and supplies

Cutting

1. Cut two 2½" x 21" A strips from each 2½" x 42" coordinating strip to total 24 A strips.

2. Cut one 2½" by fabric width strip black solid; subcut strip into two 2½" x 21" B strips.

3. Cut three 2½" by fabric width strips black solid for binding.

4. Cut one 13" by fabric width strip black solid; subcut strip into two 13" x 20½" C pillow-back pieces.

5. Cut (48) ¾" x 21" batting strips.

Completing the Pillow Top

1. Fold ¼" under along both long edges of each A and B strip as shown in Figure 1; press.

Figure 1

2. Place an A strip wrong side up on your ironing surface. Center and layer a ¾" x 21" batting strip on the wrong side of the A strip as shown in Figure 2; fold the long edges of the A strip over the batting, butting the edges in the center, again referring to Figure 2. Press to hold. Repeat with the remaining A and B strips.

Figure 2

3. Using a wide zigzag stitch or decorative stitch that moves from side to side, stitch along the center of the batted strips to hold the butted edges together as shown in Figure 3.

Figure 3

4. Using the side without the butted edges as the right side, measure 3¾" from each end of the strips and make a mark on the right side as shown in Figure 4.

Figure 4

5. Select an A strip. Place a B strip on top of the A strip with one edge of B aligned with one 3¾" mark as shown in Figure 5; pin in place. Repeat at the 3¾" mark on the other end of the A strip, again referring to Figure 5.

Figure 5

6. Place the second A strip with one long edge butted against the edge of the first A strip, placing the strip on top of the B strips and aligning the 3¾" marks with the edge of the B strips as shown in Figure 6; pin the B strips in place.

Figure 6

7. Stitch along the butted edges of the two A strips as in step 3, stopping and locking stitches at the edge of the first B strip as shown in Figure 7; begin sewing again at the opposite edge of the B strip, again referring to Figure 7. Stitch to the edge of the second B strip, skip over the B strip and stitch to the end of the butted A strips. **Note:** *The B strips are being woven into the A strips and are loose on A.*

Figure 7

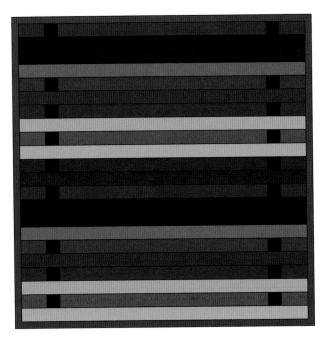

Skins & Sticks Pillow
Placement Diagram 20" x 20"

8. Repeat steps 6 and 7 to add the remaining A strips, placing the third A strip below the B strips, the fourth on top of the B strips, etc., to weave the A and B strips together.

9. Stitch along the edges of the B strips from the top to the bottom of the pieced section (Figure 8).

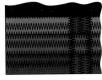

Figure 8

10. Trim the pieced section to 20½" x 20½" to complete the pillow top.

Completing the Pillow

1. Turn and press ¼" to the wrong side on one 20½" edge of both C pieces. Turn and press another ½" to wrong side and edgestitch to hem.

2. Place the pillow top right side down on a flat surface. Place the C pieces wrong sides together with the pillow top, overlapping the hemmed edges to match the size of the pillow top as shown in Figure 9. Pin outside edges to hold.

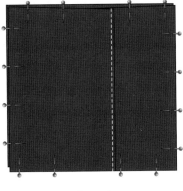

Figure 9

3. Machine-baste around outside edges through all layers using a ⅛" seam allowance.

4. Join binding strips on short ends with diagonal seams to make one long strip; trim seams to ¼" and press seams open.

5. Fold the binding strip in half with wrong sides together along length; press.

6. Sew binding to pillow edges, matching raw edges, mitering corners and overlapping ends.

7. Fold binding to the back side and stitch in place to finish. ■

3-D Tumbling Blocks

Triangles and squares create the illusion of a stretched Tumbling Block design.

DESIGN BY MARIA UMHEY

PROJECT SPECIFICATIONS

Skill Level: Beginner
Quilt Size: 54" x 60"
Block Size: 6" x 6"
Number of Blocks: 76

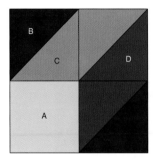

3-D Boxes
6" x 6" Block
Make 42

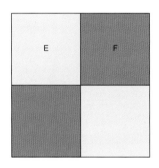

4-Patch
6" x 6" Block
Make 34

PROJECT NOTE

For each block you will need one square each light, medium and dark fabric in one color family in addition to a background square. The same fabric should be used throughout for the background. In the quilt shown, the fabric is navy solid.

Color families represented are red, brown, green and blue in varying shades of each color.

This is the perfect quilt in which to use scraps you have collected over the years.

MATERIALS

- ⅓ yard total each light red and light green
- ⅓ yard total each medium red and medium green
- ⅓ yard total each dark red and dark green
- ½ yard total each light blue and light brown
- ½ yard total each medium blue and medium brown
- ½ yard total each dark blue and dark brown
- 1⅝ yards navy solid
- Backing 60" x 66"
- Batting 60" x 66"
- Neutral color all-purpose thread
- Quilting thread
- Basic sewing tools and supplies

Cutting

1. Cut seven 3½" A squares and (12) 3½" E squares from each light red and light green.

2. Cut seven 3⅞" squares from each medium red and medium green. Cut each square on one diagonal to make 14 C triangles from each color.

3. Cut (12) 3½" F squares from each medium red and medium green.

4. Cut seven 3⅞" squares from each dark red and dark green. Cut each square on one diagonal to make 14 D triangles from each color.

5. Cut (12) 3½" G squares from each dark red and dark green.

6. Cut (14) 3½" A squares and (12) 3½" E squares from each light blue and light brown.

7. Cut (14) 3⅞" squares from each medium blue and medium brown. Cut each square on one diagonal to make 28 C triangles from each color.

8. Cut (14) 3½" F squares from each medium blue and medium brown.

9. Cut (14) 3⅞" squares from each dark blue and dark brown. Cut each square on one diagonal to make 28 D triangles from each color.

10. Cut (12) 3½" G squares from each dark blue and dark brown.

11. Cut four 3⅞" by fabric width strips from solid navy; subcut strips into (42) 3⅞" squares. Cut each square on one diagonal to make 84 B triangles.

12. Cut two 3½" x 36½" H strips and three 3½" x 42" I strips from solid navy.

13. Cut six 2¼" by fabric width strips from solid navy for binding.

Completing the 3-D Boxes Blocks

1. Select two each same-fabric medium blue C, dark blue D and navy B triangles and one light blue A square.

2. Sew B to C, B to D and C to D to make one each B-C, B-D and C-D unit as shown in Figure 1; press seams toward darker fabric.

Figure 1

3. Sew A to the D side of the B-D unit as shown in Figure 2; press seam toward A.

Figure 2

4. Join the C-D unit and the B-C unit on the C sides as shown in Figure 3; press seam toward the C-D unit.

Figure 3

5. Join the two pieced units to complete one blue 3-D Boxes block as shown in Figure 4; press seam in one direction. Repeat to make 14 blue blocks.

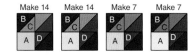

Figure 4

6. Repeat to make seven each red and green blocks and 14 brown blocks, again referring to Figure 4.

Completing the Four-Patch Blocks

1. Select two each same-fabric E and same-fabric F squares.

2. Join one E and one F square to make a row; repeat to make two rows. Press seams toward F squares.

3. Join the rows to complete one E-F Four-Patch block referring to Figure 5; press seams in one direction. Repeat to complete four E-F blocks.

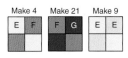

Figure 5

4. Repeat steps 1–3 to complete 21 F-G blocks, again referring to Figure 5.

5. Repeat steps 1–3 to complete nine E-E blocks, again referring to Figure 5.

Completing the Quilt

1. Arrange and join six 3-D Boxes blocks to make a row as shown in Figure 6; repeat to make seven rows. Press seams in adjoining rows in opposite directions.

Figure 6

2. Join the rows referring to the Placement Diagram to complete the pieced center; press seams in one direction.

3. Join the I strips on short ends to make one long strip; press seams open. Subcut strip into two 48½" I strips.

4. Sew H strips to the top and bottom and I strips to opposite long sides of the pieced center; press seams toward H and I strips.

5. Arrange and join the Four-Patch blocks to make two side strips with eight blocks each and a top and bottom strip with nine blocks each, placing the colors so that the lower left corner has blocks of light value and the upper right corner has blocks of dark value. Arrange the blocks to create a progression of color from light to dark emanating from these two corners. Press seams in one direction.

6. Sew the border strips to the sides, top and bottom of the pieced center to complete the pieced top; press seams toward H and I strips.

7. Press quilt top on both sides; check for proper seam pressing and trim all loose threads.

8. Sandwich batting between the stitched top and the prepared backing piece; pin or baste layers together to hold. Quilt on marked lines and as desired by hand or machine.

9. When quilting is complete, remove pins or basting. Trim batting and backing fabric edges even with raw edges of quilt top.

10. Join binding strips on short ends with diagonal seams to make one long strip; trim seams to ¼" and press seams open.

11. Fold the binding strip in half with wrong sides together along length; press.

12. Sew binding to quilt edges, matching raw edges, mitering corners and overlapping ends.

13. Fold binding to the back side and stitch in place to finish. ■

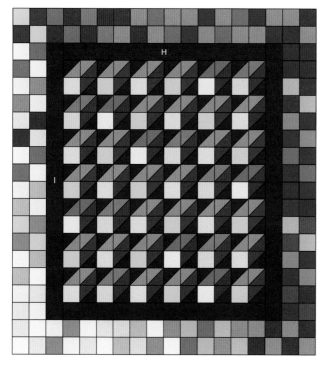

3-D Tumbling Blocks
Placement Diagram 54" x 60"

Jolly Santa Pot Holder

Continued from page 88

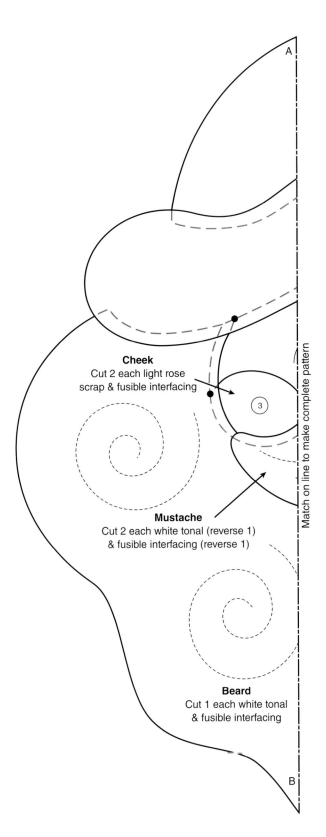

A

Cheek
Cut 2 each light rose
scrap & fusible interfacing

③

Mustache
Cut 2 each white tonal (reverse 1)
& fusible interfacing (reverse 1)

Match on line to make complete pattern

Beard
Cut 1 each white tonal
& fusible interfacing

B

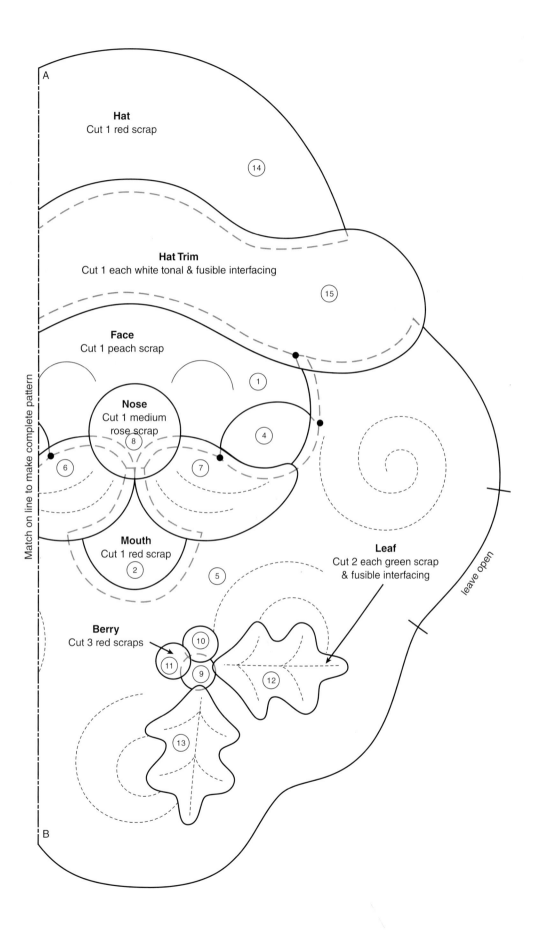

Hat
Cut 1 red scrap

14

Hat Trim
Cut 1 each white tonal & fusible interfacing

15

Face
Cut 1 peach scrap

Match on line to make complete pattern

1

Nose
Cut 1 medium
rose scrap

8

4

6

7

Mouth
Cut 1 red scrap

2

5

Leaf
Cut 2 each green scrap
& fusible interfacing

leave open

Berry
Cut 3 red scraps

10

11

9

12

13

Fabric & Supplies

Page 15: Granny's Hanky—EQ Printables and Lite Steam-A-Seam 2.

Page 27: Sassy Slide—Urban Angel by Studio E.

Page 30: Christmas Card Holder—Vintage Holiday Fabric collection from Exclusively Quilters; Machine 60/40 Blend batting from Fairfield Processing, Star Machine Quilting thread from Coats and Quilt Basting Spray from Sullivans.

Page 74: Daisy Pocket Quilt—Kids Go Green fabric collection from Quilting Treasures, Steam-A-Seam 2 fusible web and Warm & Natural cotton batting from The Warm Company, blendables multicolored thread from Sulky of America and Dual Duty XP all-purpose thread from Coats.

Page 98: Black Lily Bag—Manzanita fabric collection by Joel Dewberry for Westminster Fibers.

Page 114: Batiks Squared—Master Piece 45 ruler and Static Stickers from Master Piece Products.

Page 140: Diamond Candy—Batik fabrics from Diamond Textiles.

Page 154: Windflowers—Hobbs Thermore batting.

Page 160: Skins & Stones Throw—Stonehenge and Stonehenge Skins collection from Northcott and Star Machine Quilting thread from Coats.

Page 166: Skins & Sticks Pillow—Stonehenge and Stonehenge Skins collection from Northcott and Star Machine Quilting thread from Coats.

Special Thanks

Please join us in thanking the talented designers below.

Joan Ballard
Dots Done Your Way, 94

Karen Blocher
Sassy Slide, 27

Sandy Boobar
Skins & Sticks Pillow, 166
Skins & Stones Throw, 160

Jean Boyd
Granny's Hanky, 15

Barbara Clayton
Jolly Santa Pot Holder, 87
Puppy Dog Tails, 145
Sleepytime Lambs Baby Quilt, 126

Phyllis Dobbs
Daisy Pocket Quilt, 74

Lucy Fazely
3-D Drunkard's Path Quilt, 106
Simply Scrappy Place Mats, 50

Gina Gempesaw
Pathways Prayer Shawl, 90

Sandra L. Hatch
Christmas Card Holder, 30
Wild Goose Chase Tote, 53
Wild Goose Chase Wallet, 58

Sue Harvey
Skins & Sticks Pillow, 166
Skins & Stones Throw, 160

Sue Kim
Black Lily Bag, 98

Connie Kauffman
Strip-Pieced Place Mats, 36

Kate Laucomer
Cellphone Carrier, 79
Chair Chatelaine, 46
Friendship Stars Backpack, 136
May Day Tulip Place Mat, 68

Chris Malone
Butterfly Pot Holder, 18
Button Checkerboard, 118
Charming Coasters, 7
Halloween Treat Bags, 10
Mini Dresden Ornament, 38
Ruffled Rose Pillow, 42

Connie Rand
Color Wheel Runner 83

Cindi Rang
Diamond Candy, 140

Jill Reber
Batiks Squared, 114
E-Reader Tech Bag, 102

Marian Shenk
Fruit Quartet Pot Holders, 22

Ruth Swasey
Cracker Box, 64

Maria Umhey
3-D Tumbling Blocks, 170

Carolyn S. Vagts
Quick Mug Rugs, 34

Jodi G. Warner
Log Cabin Doll Quilt, 110

Julie Weaver
Windflowers, 154

Beth Wheeler
Pocket Full of Posies, 4

Mary Wilbur
Twisted Rail Fence, 122

Bea Yurkerwich
Magic Maze, 132